A World Premiere
A Live Theatre Production

By Ron Hutchinson

Based on an original story by Victoria Fischer

Live Theatre, Newcastle
Thursday 27 November to Saturday 20 December 2014

The first performance of *Flying Into Daylight* was
at Live Theatre on Thursday 27 November 2014.

Supported by the Friends of Live Theatre

A Word From The Writer

ONE

The two competing theories of evolution are that progress and change occur steadily and, alternatively, that everything goes along much as it always has until one day the roof falls in. Coming from Northern Ireland, I'm genetically and temperamentally pre-disposed to believe in the roof-falling-in theory of history; in personal affairs as well as public.

That's why I was so taken with the life experience of Victoria Fischer, who inspired this play. An actor in another of my plays, she responded, when asked by the director to outline a moment or decision that fundamentally changed things, by talking of going to Buenos Aires to learn the Tango. Out of the blue. Without a word of Spanish. Just knowing that some force inside her was telling her to do it. Now.

Soon I was to discover that she wasn't alone in feeling that impulse – or interior command – and obeying; without question but certainly with apprehension. Argentina's a long way away. They beat us regularly at football and we have a continuing political disagreement with them. No matter. People, like Victoria, of every age and nationality and class, wake up one morning and decide that whatever else their life contains, it must have room for a studio or bar or nightclub or ballroom thousands of miles away. On the floor of that distant place they will learn Tango.

TWO

In the days when you could get to Australia on the Assisted Passage Scheme for ten pounds, my parents had their bags packed, ready to leave Belfast for a new life. Blue skies. Sunshine. A guaranteed job for my dad, a brickie, at a good wage. At the last minute my mother backed out. She had four sisters and didn't want to leave them so far away. The moment was there when their lives could have changed for ever. They argued. He lost. She won. They both lost.

They stayed together for another fifty years but I know that the bitterness of his failure to talk/force her into getting on the boat was sharp in his side as he lay on the bed he died in. I know that he never forgave her or himself. I know that in many ways his life hadn't lasted the ninety three years it said on his death certificate; the fifty years he spent working on the buildings; the eight years he spent in the RAF. It had lasted until the moment he paused in his anger and then shrugged and said '*Have it your way, missus.*' In that half second he undid his life.

THREE

A Femtosecond is a measurement of time equal to 10^{-15} of a second. That is one quadrillionth, or one millionth of one billionth, of a second. Which means it's in proportion to one of your average seconds as that average second is to thirty two million years. Scientists use it on a daily basis. When you think how many Femtoseconds your life therefore contains (70 x 365 x 24 x 60 x 60 x 1,000,000,000,000,000,000,000,000) it doesn't seem such a bad deal. Plenty of time to fix the gutters, learn Italian, read *War and Peace* or learn the Tango.

FOUR

As a writer I spend most of my time in a web of words. My interest in dance as an art form that uses a different language to express the truth I look for was sparked by the work of Richard Buckle. A ballet critic and outrageous, larger than life character, he behaved with conspicuous bravery – and eccentricity – in the Second World War. In the bloody Italian campaign he refused to lie down under shellfire so that he wouldn't get mud on his uniform. When his regiment liberated a town after a brutal hand to hand fight he went into it alone, ignoring the snipers still there and emerged with several old books, many of them pornographic and a wedding dress which he wore that night at dinner.

I still remember his paragraph in an *Observer* review that made me think that dance in general and ballet in particular might be worth looking into. In it he expressed his astonishment that educated, cultured people could be unaware of the existence of one of the true creative geniuses of the twentieth century – George Balanchine. I'd never heard the name. It was one not bandied about in Coventry, where we'd moved to after Belfast.

I discovered another way of being when I started to learn about Balanchine and his work and I'm very conscious that we are pre-miering this play in a theatre so strongly associated with Lee Hall. His *Billy Elliot* threw open so many other windows for so many people who might not otherwise have found their way to that extraordinary, profound, joyous and demanding art.

FIVE

On second thoughts, perhaps not even 2,207,520,000,000,000, 000,000,000,000,000,000 Femtoseconds would be enough to learn and perfect all the varieties of Tango – *anyenque, orillero, salon, milonguero, nuevo, tradicional, con corte y quebrada* and *fantasia*. Better start now. Tonight. After the show.

SIX

Most of my writing life has been spent in Hollywood; where I'm continually surprised at how ready audiences are to pay to see the same movies, stories and characters re-imagined and sometimes totally re-invented. Maybe that's not just creative exhaustion but speaks to an endless human fascination with the possibility of personal change. Most of us are stuck with the personas and lives we've created, even if we are, consciously or not, living a fictionalized version of ourselves. It's great to believe that we could start again with a clean sheet.

In the form of Tango I write about in the play, the dance floor is always a clean sheet; the dancers being required not to follow a set series of steps but to continually experiment and improvise, without words or pre-arrangement. It combines Performance and Invention; Mind and Body; Desire and Technique; our need for order in the part of ourselves that acknowledges Apollo and the need for ecstatic release in the service of Dionysus; offering those caught in the spell of its music new perspectives on themselves, new ways of being and the always present possibility of finding our true selves…but only if we are brave enough to take that first step when the moment of decision arrives and walk onto the dance floor…

Ron Hutchinson
Writer & Co-Director

The Original Story by Victoria Fischer

In September 2010, I made my way to a friend's house in South London to learn the basic steps of Argentine Tango. I arrived apprehensive with preconceptions based on Tango I had seen on television – an abundance of passion, satin and leg – but here I was about to experience something at odds with my very British nature. My friend and I stood in socks on the kitchen floor. He took my right hand, touched my back with his other and we walked, in time together around the room with an orchestra accompanying our steps, violins, pianos and the deep guttural sounds of the bandoneon.

Two weeks later, I was 7,000 miles from home, at Buenos Aires International airport, praying that the impulsive trip to learn Argentine Tango in its heartland was not a mistake. However, over the next few months I realised that any fear I had of travelling alone was blown out of the water by the fear of stepping onto a dance floor in front of hundreds of strangers every night. Tango was not for the faint-hearted and here, congregating daily in dance studios across the city, I found something transcendent that welcomed all ages and nationalities into its embrace. Including this young British woman.

Returning home after three months, I felt like a foreigner in my own country. From the raucous streets of Buenos Aires I had dropped back into quiet, suburban Buckinghamshire; a scene change that couldn't have been more jarring. Finding it difficult to move back to my daily routine – and with Andrew Lloyd Webber's *Don't Cry for Me Argentina* playing on repeat – I created a one-woman show, building on a blog I'd kept whilst away, and relived the moments I had experienced there.

Just as Tango appeared so swiftly into my life, two years later the story captured the imagination of a writer, Ron Hutchinson, and we began to create a full play from my adventure. Every Argentine Tango dancer, be it a beginner or a world champion, has a personal story to tell of how they came to find this dance, or as in my case, how it found *them*. Across the globe from Paris to Havana, Siberia to India there are thousands of dancers who discover that once they start learning, it becomes an addiction they cannot stop. Tango is just an improvised set of steps, but it becomes a compulsion that inexplicably grips certain individuals and compels them to travel alone across the world, to spend hundreds of hours in lessons and at social dances (*milongas*).

Over the last century Argentine Tango has continued to evolve in style and the number of dancers is constantly increasing, yet there are still very few studies, books or plays on the dance. *Flying Into Daylight* will be the first of its kind in combining Tango dance and bandoneon music in a theatrical form and it's thanks to Ron's magnificent skills as a writer, that having never danced one step of Tango he can express so simply and beautifully Virginia's journey into that world. The play is not based solely on my experience; it is the passage of so many people also in search of that very human desire for change.

I am thrilled that this story is receiving its premiere at Live Theatre with a hugely talented cast and creative team and I hope that for a few hours, you too can feel the energy, escapism and vitality of Buenos Aires and Argentine Tango.

Victoria Fischer
Original Story

A Word From Live Theatre's Artistic Director

I hadn't met Ron Hutchinson before this project came about. I'd been aware of his early stage work over here and in the United States but our paths had never crossed until last year when a mutual friend, Eoin O'Callaghan read the first draft of *Flying Into Daylight* and put us both in touch.

Eoin made a good call. I read it, loved it and thought we should try and make it happen. The script was beautifully written, based on a true story by Victoria Fischer, cradled within a clever overall metaphor that I found both sensual and life-affirming.

The exciting possibility of fusing the art form of Tango, with its distinctive choreography and live music seemed to my mind inherently theatrical. It looked a perfect fit for Live Theatre but at the same time like many of our plays, had a universal reach; from Tyneside to London and New York via Newcastle Quayside and the docklands of Buenos Aires.

In creating this piece we are delighted to welcome back some of our most talented creative associates, Gary McCann as Designer and Malcolm Rippeth as Lighting Designer along with two of the country's finest exponents of the Tango art form, bandoneonist and composer Julian Rowlands and choreographer Amir Giles who come to Live Theatre for the first time.

The casting of Summer Strallen and Jos Vantyler completes an ensemble of enormous and glittering talent who, along with our brilliant production team and the entire staff of Live Theatre, aim to give our audiences a great night out in the theatre. And finally not forgetting our Friends of Live Theatre whose support continues to help us do all we do, and whose support we are acknowledging alongside this World Premiere of *Flying Into Daylight*.

Thanks to them all. Enjoy.

Max Roberts
Co-Director & Artistic Director, **Live Theatre**

Cast

Virginia **Summer Strallen**

Marco **Jos Vantyler**

Creative & Production Team

Writer **Ron Hutchinson**

Based on an original story by **Victoria Fischer**

Directors **Ron Hutchinson & Max Roberts**

Music created & performed by **Julian Rowlands**

Choreographer **Amir Giles**

Designer **Gary McCann**

Lighting Designer **Malcolm Rippeth**

Sound Designer & Technical Manager **David Flynn**

Production Manager **Drummond Orr**

Creative Producer **Graeme Thompson**

Stage Manager **Fiona Kennedy**

Deputy Stage Manager **Kate McCheyne**

Technician **Sam Stewart**

Creative Apprentice **Craig Spence**

Costume Supervisor **Lou Duffy**

Assistant Choreographer **Tara Pilbrow**

Casting **Sooki McShane CDG**

Casting **Lucy Jenkins CDG**

For Assisted Performances

British Sign Language **Caroline Ryan**

Captioning **Philip Armstrong**

Audio Description & Touch Tour **Louise Ainsley**

Thanks

Naomi Grant, for her advice on Francis Bacon, Miranda Garrison and Leandro Palou for their help with the initial workshop in London, Eoin O'Callaghan, Aaron Davies for use of his photograph for the initial image, Lee Proud and Michelle Percy at Silverlink Holdings.

CAST

Virginia **Summer Strallen**

Theatre credits include: *The Life of the Party – A Celebration of the Songs of Andrew Lippa* (Menier Chocolate Factory), Dale Tremont in *Top Hat* (Aldwych Theatre and National Tour), for which she received her fourth Olivier Award Nomination for 2013 Best Actress in a Musical, Meg Giry in *Love Never Dies* (Adelphi Theatre), for which she received a 2011 Olivier Award Nomination for Best Performance in a Supporting Role in a Musical, *Company* (Queen's Theatre) directed by Jamie Lloyd, *Paradise Moscow* (Opera North) directed by David Pountney, Maria in *The Sound of Music* (London Palladium), Janet Van Der Graaf in *The Drowsy Chaperone* (Novello Theatre), for which she received a 2008 Olivier Award Nomination for Best Actress in a Musical, *Dick Whittington* (Barbican Theatre) directed by Edward Hall, Maisie in *The Boyfriend* (Open Air Theatre, Regent's Park) and received a 2007 Olivier Award Nomination for Best Supporting Role in a Musical, *A Midsummer Night's Dream* (Open Air Theatre, Regent's Park), *Guys and Dolls* (Piccadilly Theatre) directed by Michael Grandage, *Chitty Chitty Bang Bang* (London Palladium), *Cats* (New London Theatre and National Tour), *Fosse* (European Tour), *Anything Goes* (Grange Park Opera), *Scrooge* (Dominion Theatre) and *The Sound of Music* (Sadler's Wells).

Television and film credits include: *Casualty* (BBC), *Five-Aside* (Emerald Films), *Doctors* (BBC), *The Land Girls* (BBC), *Hotel Babylon* (Carnival Films), *Beyond The Sea* directed by Kevin Spacey and *Hollyoaks* (Lime Pictures).

Workshops include: *Marilyn* directed by David Grindley and *It's A Wonderful Life.*

Recordings include: *Top Hat* (Original Cast Album) and *Love Never Dies* (Concept Album).

Marco **Jos Vantyler**

Jos Vantyler won a Theatre Choice Award for Outstanding Performance in a new play and was nominated a second time for an OffWestEnd Award (Offie) for Best Male Performance of 2012 for his portrayal of the promoter of the Dance Marathon contest in *Dead on Her Feet*, also written by Ron Hutchinson.

He appeared in the all-star cast of *King Lear* at The Old Vic in 2013 and in *Love's Labours Lost* for the 20th anniversary of Northern Broadsides in 2011. He learnt the Trapeze to play the protagonist of *Circus Britannica* in 2011 (The Bike Shed Theatre). He played Tom Sawyer in James Graham's *Huck* (Southwalk Playhouse and National Tour) and received an Offie nomination for Outstanding Male Performance. Other award-winning and nominated work includes *Ghosts* by Henrik Ibsen (Lincoln Center, New York), *A View From the Bridge* by Arthur Miller (New York Tower Productions) and the Broadway transfer of *Prophecy* (New End Theatre).

On television he has appeared on *Knight Spell* and the *Name of God* (Fairmont/HBO) and *Here and Now* (CBS).

CREATIVE TEAM

Ron Hutchinson
Writer & Co-Director

Writer Ron Hutchinson is an Emmy award-winning screenwriter for *Murderers Among Us: The Simon Wiesenthal Story*, currently based in Los Angeles. He has received four other Emmy nominations. After working at several jobs, including carpet fitter, fish gutter and Social Security Department fraud investigator, he wrote his first television play *Twelve Off The Belt* for the BBC. A series of television plays and series then followed, including two series of *Bird of Prey* starring the late Richard Griffiths and *Connie*, starring Stephanie Beecham.

Ron's first stage play, *Says I Says He*, was produced at the Sheffield Crucible, Royal Court Theatre and Mark Taper Forum, Los Angeles. It led to his becoming Writer In Residence at the Royal Shakespeare Company and won him the George Devine Award. Other plays that have been produced internationally include *Moonlight and Magnolias* at The Goodman Theatre, Chicago, The Tricycle and the Manhattan Theatre Club which was nominated for the 2004 Joseph Jefferson Award for New Work in Chicago and won a New York Critic's Circle Comedy Award. West End productions include Steven Daldry's revival of *Rat in the Skull* (Olivier Award nomination) and *Beau Brummel* at the Haymarket, Leicester Square. For the Royal National Theatre he adapted Mikhail Bulgakov's *Flight* and Carl Zuckmayer's *The Captain of Kopenick*, both performed on the Olivier stage.

After moving to Los Angeles he wrote and produced extensively for American cable and network companies including HBO, ABC, NBC, CBS, Lifetime and Showtime. He has recently resumed writing for BBC radio and his series of five short plays, *Hollywood Endings* starring Kathleen Turner, is due for transmission on BBC Radio 4 in 2014. He has also taught screenwriting at the American Film Institute in Los Angeles.

Victoria Fischer

Original Story

Victoria trained at The Oxford School of Drama. Her first play *Finding Evita*, based on her journey to Buenos Aires to learn Tango, debuted at the Face to Face Solo Theatre Festival in London in 2012. She developed this play with Ron Hutchinson; *Flying Into Daylight* is the result of that collaboration.

Other theatre credits include roles in *Backbeat* at Citizens Theatre, Glasgow; *Dead on Her Feet* at The North Wall, Oxford and Arcola Theatre in London and a UK Tour as Juliet in *Romeo and Juliet* with the Young Shakespeare Company.

Max Roberts

Co-Director

Max is the Artistic Director and a founding member of Live Theatre. His directing credits include new plays by some of the finest writers from the North East including: CP Taylor, Tom Hadaway, Alan Plater, Phil Woods, Julia Darling, Shelagh Stephenson, Peter Straughan, Lee Hall and Michael Chaplin.

For Live Theatre's 40th anniversary season in 2013 Max directed *Tyne* by Michael Chaplin, *Wet House* by Paddy Campbell and a revival of Lee Hall's *Cooking with Elvis*, a play he first directed for Live Theatre 16 years ago. In 2014, Max directed a series of rehearsed readings of screenplays by Lee Hall (and Simon Beaufoy) as well as Live Theatre's new production *Good Timin'* and *Wet House* which returned to Live Theatre before going on a National Tour.

Julian Rowlands

Musical Composer & Performer

Julian Rowlands, one of Europe's leading Tango musicians, is a bandoneonist, composer and arranger specialising in Tango, classical and contemporary music. Julian received his degree in music from Southampton University and studied bandoneon with the leading Argentinean player Victor Villena.
Julian is a member of *Tango Siempre*, and created the

score for the Olivier Award nominated show *Midnight Tango* together with Ros Stephen and Jonathan Taylor of *Tango Siempre*. He performed in the show in the West End and on tour from 2011 to 2013.

He has appeared on BBC television's *Strictly Come Dancing*, *The One Show* and *Zingzillas*, on BBC Radio 3's *In Tune*, and at major concert and theatre venues in the UK and Europe such as the Wigmore Hall, Queen Elizabeth Hall, the Royal Opera House and the Phoenix and Aldwych Theatres.

Amir Giles
Choreographer

Amir Giles is a performer and choreographer, who trained at the Rambert School of Ballet and Contemporary Dance. His experience spans performance, collaborative devising, movement direction and choreography for television, film, theatre and opera.

He has taught at The Royal Ballet School, The Royal College of Music, *Bodyguard – The Musical*, The Royal Ballet, for productions at the Royal Opera House and the Royal Albert Hall, and multiple major Tango schools in London and abroad. As a choreographer and movement director Amir has worked with Paramount Pictures, Boy George, Film4 and The Royal College of Music.

He has appeared in roles as a swing dancer in Marvel Comics' Avenger's sequel, as Señor Gomerez in ITV's *Mr Selfridge* and in a collaboration with *Strictly Come Dancing*'s Nicole Cutler.

Gary McCann
Designer

Originally from County Armagh, Northern Ireland, Gary trained at Nottingham Trent University, and is now based in Greenwich, London.

His design credits for theatre and opera include: *The Pitmen Painters* (Live Theatre, National Theatre London, Volkstheater

Vienna, Friedman Theatre Broadway, Bill Kenwright tour and Duchess Theatre), *The Girl in the Yellow Dress* (Live Theatre, Market Theatre Johannesburg, Stadttheater Stockholm, Baxter Theatre, Cape Town), *The Barber of Seville*, *La Voix Humaine*, *L'Heure Espagnole* (Nationale Reisopera, Holland), *Die Fledermaus* (Norwegian National Opera), *The Flying Dutchman* (Ekaterinburg State Opera, Russia), *Three Days in May*, *Dangerous Corner* (Bill Kenwright), *33 Variations* (Volkstheater Vienna), *Guys and Dolls* (Theater Bielefeld, Germany), *Fidelio* (Garsington Opera), *Cosi Fan Tutte* (Schönbrunn Palace, Vienna), *Norma* (National Opera of Moldova), *Imeneo* (London Handel Festival), *Faramondo* (Göttingen Festspiele Germany), *Owen Wingrave* and *La Pietra Del Paragone* (Opera Trionfo, Amsterdam).

Current engagements include commissions for Vienna State Opera, Santa Fe Opera, New Mexico, Nationale Reisopera Holland, National Opera Bucharest, Dallas Opera and the Hobart Baroque Festival, Tazmania. His work has been exhibited at the V&A Museum in London twice – as part of the *Collaborators* and *Transformation/Revelation* exhibitions.

Malcolm Rippeth
Lighting Designer

Malcolm's previous shows at Live Theatre include *Keepers of the Flame*, *A Nightingale Sang in Eldon Square* and *Toast*.

Other work includes: *The Bloody Chamber* (Northern Stage), *Rapunzel* (balletLORENT), *West Side Story* (Sage Gateshead), *The Empress* (RSC), *The Promise* (Donmar Warehouse), *Spur of The Moment* (Royal Court), *Spring Awakening* (Headlong), *Stones in his Pockets* (Tricycle Theatre), *The Night Before Christmas* (Soho Theatre), *The Dead* (Abbey, Dublin), *The Birthday Party* (Royal Exchange Theatre), *London* (Paines Plough), *Ghost From A Perfect Place* (Arcola Theatre), *Forever House* (Theatre Royal Plymouth), *The Threepenny Opera* (Graeae), *Refugee Boy* (West Yorkshire Playhouse), *His Dark Materials* (Birmingham Rep), *Moon Tiger* (Theatre Royal Bath), *Calendar Girls* (West End/Australia/Canada), *HMS Pinafore* (Guthrie Theater Minneapolis), *Copenhagen* (Royal Lyceum,

Edinburgh), *The Coronation of Poppea* (Opera North), *Orfeo ed Euridice* (Buxton Festival), *Le Nozze di Figaro* (Garsington Opera) and *Seven Deadly Sins* (WNO). He is an Associate Artist of Kneehigh Theatre, productions including *Tristan & Yseult*, *The Wild Bride*, *The Umbrellas of Cherbourg* and *Brief Encounter* (West End/Broadway/Australia).

Lucy Jenkins & Sooki McShane CDG

Casting

Live Theatre credits include: *Tyne*, *Cooking with Elvis*, *Chalet Lines*, *A Walk On Part*, *Nativities*, *Faith & Cold Reading*, *Inheritance* and *A Northern Odyssey*.

Other theatre credits include: *To Kill a Mockingbird* (Regents Park and tour), *The Man Who Shot Liberty Valance*, *Desdemona*, *Bomber's Moon*, *Adult Supervision* and *Casualties* (Park Theatre), *Our Country's Good* (Out Of Joint), *Much Ado About Nothing* (Royal Exchange Theatre), *Moon on a Rainbow Shawl* (Talawa Theatre), *War Horse* (UK Tour/West End), *Solid Air* (Theatre Royal Plymouth), *Afraid of the Dark* (Charing Cross Theatre), *Serpent's Tooth* (Almeida Theatre/Talawa Theatre), *The Glee Club* (Cast Theatre) and several productions for Nottingham Playhouse including *The Kite Runner*, *My Judy Garland Life*, *Richard III*, *The Ashes* and *Diary of a Football Nobody*.

Television credits include: *Skins* (Company Pictures), *Wild At Heart* (Company Pictures), *The Bill* (Talkback Thames), *Samuel Johnson: The Dictionary Man* (October Films) and *Family Affairs* (Talkback Thames).

Film credits include: *Myrrdin* (Screenworks), *Awaiting* (Solar Productions), *Containment* (Bright Cold Day Films), *Five-A-Side* (Emerald Films), *Entity* (Nexus DNA), *The Somnambulists* (No Bad Films), *Desi Boyz* (Desi Boyz Productions) and *H10* (Dan Films).

About Live Theatre

From its base on Newcastle's quayside, Live Theatre produces work as varied and diverse as the audiences it engages with. To do this it:

- Creates and performs new plays of world class quality
- Finds and develops creative talent
- Unlocks the potential of young people through theatre.

Founded in 1973, the Theatre was transformed in 2007 with a capital redevelopment. The result is a beautifully restored and refurbished complex of five Grade II listed buildings with state-of-the-art facilities in a unique historical setting, including a 160-seat cabaret-style theatre, a studio theatre, renovated rehearsal rooms, a series of dedicated writers' rooms as well as a thriving café, bar and pub.

Live Theatre is a national leader in developing new strategies for increasing income and assets for the charity. In 2014 the company announced LiveWorks, a £10 million capital development to purchase and develop quayside-fronted land and buildings adjacent to the Theatre, to create a children and young people's writing centre, a public park and new commercial office space.

LiveWorks will join the award-winning gastro pub The Broad Chare, online course www.beaplaywright.com and The Schoolhouse (office space for emerging businesses), as one of Live Theatre's creative enterprises designed to increase income.

For more information see www.live.org.uk

Through the generosity of our Friends Live Theatre is able to continue to nurture and develop new writing talent, and deliver plays of world class quality. Our Best Friends are:

Noreen Bates
Jim Beirne
Michael & Pat Brown
Paul Callaghan
George Caulkin
Michael & Susan Chaplin
Sue & Simon Clugston
Helen Coyne
Chris Foy
Robson Green
Lee Hall
John Jordan
John Josephs
Annette Marlowe
Madelaine Newton
Elaine Orrick
Ian & Christine Shepherdson
Margaret & John Shipley
Sting
Shelagh Stephenson
Peter Straughan
Alan Tailford
Graeme & Aly Thompson
Paul & Julie Tomlinson
Nick & Melanie Tulip
Alison Walton
Kevin Whately
Lucy Winskell

For more information about the Friends of Live Theatre please contact Lizzy Skingley on **(0191) 269 3499** or **lizzy@live.org.uk**

Live Theatre is grateful for the support of Arts Council England and Newcastle City Council as well as its many other supporters and Friends.

Staff at Live Theatre

Chief Executive Jim Beirne
Artistic Director Max Roberts
Operations Director Wendy Barnfather
Director of Enterprise & Development Lucy Bird
Director of Education & Engagement Helen Moore
Administrator, Directors Clare Overton
Literary Manager Gez Casey
Creative Producer Graeme Thompson
Administrator, Literary Team Degna Stone
Associate Director, Literary Team Steve Gilroy
Production Manager Drummond Orr
Technical Manager Dave Flynn
Technician Sam Stewart
Technical Apprentice Craig Spence
Associate Director, Education & Participation Paul James
Drama Worker Rachel Glover
Drama Worker Philip Hoffmann
Administrator, Education & Participation Sam Bell
Marketing Manager Claire Cockroft
Marketing Manager Cait Read
Marketing & Press Officer Emma Hall
Marketing & Press Assistant Melanie Rashbrooke
Box Office Administrator Amy Foley
Development Manager Lizzy Skingley
Events & Hires Administrator Chris Foley
Finance Manager Antony Robertson
Finance Officer Catherine Moody
Finance Assistant Helen Tuffnell
House Manager Carole Wears
Deputy House Manager Michael Davies
Duty House Manager Benjamin Young
Duty House Manager Mark Gerrens
Duty House Manager Lewis Jobson

Front of House & Box Office Staff

Phillip Barron, Nina Berry, Camille Burridge, Roisin Linton, Caroline Liversidge, Sarah Matthews, Emily Merritt, Hannah Murphy, Matilda Neill, Alisienne Petri, Tilly Riley, Anna Ryder and Molly Wright.

FLYING INTO DAYLIGHT

Ron Hutchinson

FLYING INTO DAYLIGHT

Based on an original story by Victoria Fischer

OBERON BOOKS
LONDON

WWW.OBERONBOOKS.COM

First published in 2014 by Oberon Books Ltd

521 Caledonian Road, London N7 9RH

Tel: +44 (0) 20 7607 3637 / Fax: +44 (0) 20 7607 3629

e-mail: info@oberonbooks.com

www.oberonbooks.com

A catalogue record for this book is available from the British Library.

PB ISBN: 978-1-78319-179-6

E ISBN: 978-1-78319-678-4

Cover design by Cathy Gillespie and Mark Slater Photography

Characters

MARCO

VIRGINIA

BLENNERHASSET

LARRY

HISTORY TEACHER

JOCK

PLUMBER

TAXI DRIVER

ROOFER

DENTIST

OFF LICENSE OWNER

GARAGE MECHANIC

PHIL

ALBERT

HOTEL OWNER

DOCTOR

ERIK

NEIL

CHRISTA

MUSICIAN

All the characters are played by the two actors and location changes managed without blackouts. The Bandoneon/Piano/Violin Player remains on stage, in view. He and the instruments are as much characters as those played by the actors.

Act One

The first notes of a Tango tune played by the bandoneon sound. Spotlight: we see the MUSICIAN, on stage. A man's voice.

MARCO: Tango begins in darkness, on the street where the outcasts live –

Spotlight on the Argentinian Tango teacher MARCO, with a cigarette in his hand.

MARCO: It begins with those washed up on the beaches of this great city, Buenos Aires, *la Reina del Plata*, the city of fair winds at the end of the world – those who have no country, no home, no job, no women.

The bandoneon is joined by more instruments as the music swells.

MARCO: Two men start to dance with each other. This is dangerous thing in these streets so Tango is born in danger. This is dance of the brothel – of those who lived on wrong side of the law. It is dance of desire.
Remember this.

Spotlight on the English student dancer VIRGINIA, who is wearing a prim dress, high around the collar. She carries a backpack.

MARCO: You should be afraid every time you step on dance floor because this is not dance like any other dance.

She drops the backpack as the music gets even more lush and romantic.

MARCO: It begins with *abrazo* – the embrace –

He opens his arms.

MARCO: Come to me, woman –

He throws the cigarette onto the floor and stamps it out as she walks towards him as if she can't help herself.

MARCO: Put your body against mine. Closer. Closer.
So close that you can feel my heart beating.

She does so as the music swells and he takes her in the abrazo.

MARCO: Do not move. We wait until they're beating together. Your heart and my heart. What is your name?

VIRGINIA: Vir – Virginia.

MARCO: Where are you from, Virginia?

VIRGINIA: Eng – England.

MARCO: Can you feel my heart beating, Virginia from England?

She swallows and nods.

MARCO: I feel your heart. It is cold, small English heart but I will warm it.

He pulls out a rose, puts it between her teeth and the music sweeps them into a flashy, nightclub style Tango with intricate steps and lifts.

When it ends she's on the floor, breathless with desire. With a trembling hand she offers him the rose. He takes it, twists off the head, scatters the petal.

MARCO: That is Tango.

She turns to us.

VIRGINIA: No it isn't. It really isn't. Honestly. What it is, is – well – that's what this is going to be about. Desire, yes, that'll be there and Technique, as well and a journey that isn't finished yet and – and Marco, of course.

She gets to her feet, helped by MARCO.

VIRGINIA: We'll get back to him later.

This is going to be a simple story. It's going to start in an auction house in Bond Street in London and it'll end in – I'm not sure yet.

As she straightens her dress we see images of Francis Bacon's iconic and savage depiction of the brute physicality of human bodies. She uses a laser pointer to indicate the painting as she efficiently gives us some basic facts; as if this is a lecture and we are her students.

VIRGINIA: *Three Studies For Figures At The Base of a Crucifixion* is the work in which Francis Bacon – twenty-eighth of October nineteen oh nine to the twenty-eighth of April nineteen ninety-two – first fully realized the obsessions which would project him into the front rank of twentieth-century painters; a century whose collective horrors echo in his bleak, unflinching explorations of the human body;

flayed, twisted, turned inside out; tortured, abused, pushed to the limits of what pain is bearable and then beyond it; an agonized meditation on what our physical natures can bear and a search for the seat of the soul which forever retreats and, if it is anywhere, is certainly not in the blood, gut, sinew, muscle and tissue towards which he implacably directs our unwilling but compulsive gaze.

She sets the pointer down, turns to her boss, BEN BLENNERHASSET.

VIRGINIA: Mr. Blennerhasset?

BLENNERHASSET: There's nothing wrong with the words or the ideas, Virginia but – well – when I saw my first Francis Bacon I felt a personal shock – it was overwhelming – almost obscene. The last thing it was, was an art history lesson or an abstract meditation on soul. In your piece there's a little too much head and not enough – forgive me – belly.

VIRGINIA: Belly, Mr. Blennerhasset?

BLENNERHASSET: What is the point of art if you don't take it personally? If you don't live by it and die for it, if you have to?

There's a quote of Milan Kundera's on Bacon's portraits. About filler.

VIRGINIA: Filler, Mr. Blennerhasset?

BLENNERHASSET: He says that almost all great modern artists do away with filler, with everything that comes from habit, from technical routine, whatever keeps them getting directly and exclusively at the essential – the thing the artist himself or herself and only he or she is able to say. You might want to think about that.

VIRGINIA: *(To us.)* I did. It hit me for six. As my grandfather – a Jewish refugee from Vienna in the thirties – might have said. Though when he said it he always looked a bit anxious. Could it be hit for five? Or seven?

I was thinking about it that night when I left work –

LARRY: Hold the lift!

VIRGINIA: His briefcase flew open as he got into it –

LARRY LAWLOR's briefcase flies open and a pair of men's patent leather dance shoes fall out.

VIRGINIA: Let me. Here.

LARRY: Thank you. I suppose you're wondering what –

VIRGINIA: No.

LARRY: The – ah –

VIRGINIA: Honestly, no. *(To us.)* I was intrigued, however. What on earth was –

LARRY: Larry Lawlor –

VIRGINIA: – from –

LARRY: – Accounts –

VIRGINIA: – doing with a pair of –

LARRY: – dance shoes. Patent leather. Cost a fortune –

VIRGINIA: – in his briefcase?

LARRY: Tango.

VIRGINIA: Tango?

LARRY: Ever danced it?

VIRGINIA: No.

LARRY: You've wasted your life.

VIRGINIA: I've done what?

LARRY: I go to a *milonga* three nights a week. Sometimes four or five. All over London.

VIRGINIA: *Milonga?*

A burst of cascading chords from the bandoneon; passionate and ecstatic, announcing the first moment she makes contact with Tango.

LARRY: Did a Tango Marathon in Budapest last weekend. Going to a Tango Festival in Helsinki next month.

VIRGINIA: I saw you dancing at the Office Party at Christmas –

LARRY: Office party? A Grab and a Grope. That's not Tango. Tango's –

More cascading chords of what will be a repeated musical theme throughout the play.

LARRY: Why don't you come see for yourself?

VIRGINIA: *(To us.)* I did. Forget Larry. For the time being, anyway.

She goes to a pile of chairs stacked on top of each other and starts to pull them onto the stage.

VIRGINIA: You'll meet him again at the end of this but for now he's just the accident that led me to discovering that all over London – all over the UK – all over the world, as I know now – on any night of the week, people leave the office or the shop or the house carrying dance shoes and head for Tango classes in Istanbul and Barcelona and New Jersey and Melbourne and even Nairobi, yes, Nairobi – and for Tango *milongas* in Vancouver and Moscow and Riga, Latvia – I think it's Latvia – where there are people like me or rather the person I'd suddenly become who for a few hours lose the filler in their lives – turn habit into passion – lose the boring technical requirements of ordinary life to learn the much more demanding ones of Tango which means really to get to the *essential* of something –

She and the male actor set out the chairs in an open square, individuating each new character, each one with a spike of music from the bandoneon.

VIRGINIA: I met the sad-eyed bank teller and the shifty city trader –

HISTORY TEACHER: The tweedy History teacher –

VIRGINIA: Bashful librarian –

JOCK: Morose Jock –

VIRGINIA: Dumpy cashier –

PLUMBER: Plumber –

VIRGINIA: Vet –

TAXI DRIVER: Cabbie –

VIRGINIA: Nanny –

ROOFER: Roofer –

VIRGINIA: Cook –

She sits in one of the chairs and puts her tango shoes on.

VIRGINIA: Even in the outwardly respectable Buckinghamshire village I commuted from into London every day there was a Tango Underworld. The dentist and his wife –

He puts his on, too.

DENTIST: We've been dancing Tango for years –

VIRGINIA: The couple who ran the off license –

OFF LICENSE OWNER: Twice a week, wouldn't miss it –

VIRGINIA: One of the mechanics at the local garage –

GARAGE MECHANIC: Me and the girlfriend –

VIRGINIA: It began to seem that half of the people I knew were obsessed with Tango or knew somebody who was. All of whom had heard –

The Bandoneon plays a few scattered, enticing notes as he looks up, listens.

VIRGINIA: Just as I had heard –

It sounds again and she looks up, too.

VIRGINIA: I can't explain a lot of this. Even now it's a mystery why that instrument and that music led me to such uncomfortable and dangerous places; starting with a couple of months of private lessons before I felt confident to go to my first *milonga* –

PHIL: Hang on –

VIRGINIA: Boyfriend –

PHIL: Phil Barlow – *milonga?*

VIRGINIA: On-off. Currently on. Ish.

PHIL: Pharmaceutical Sales. London and South East. *Milonga?*

VIRGINIA: Engaged, actually.

PHIL: So you sit around the side –

He indicates the chairs.

PHIL: – and the blokes size you up and –

He snaps his fingers at a chair.

PHIL: – you have to dance with a total stranger?

VIRGINIA: I can look away – which says *Please leave me alone, I won't dance with you* –

She sits and mimes that look.

VIRGINIA: Or look down – which says *I'll think about it* –

She mimes that look.

VIRGINIA: Or I'll say *Yes.*

She looks up, smiles.

PHIL: Yes, to a total stranger? *Yes* to what?

VIRGINIA: Three Tangos. Then the dance pauses for you to get your breath back and catch up with the other people there and maybe get a drink and then there's another three.

PHIL: With you sitting on the meat rack?

VIRGINIA: It's not like that.

He sits, mimes how she looked down.

PHIL: No.

He looks sideways.

PHIL: Maybe.

He stands up.

PHIL: Yes. After? What happens after?

VIRGINIA: That's it.

PHIL: There's no funny business? *How about trying a few new steps back at my place?*

VIRGINIA: I'm sure that happens. It's not why I'm there.

PHIL: Why are you there?

VIRGINIA: Why don't you come and see?

PHIL takes out a packet of cigarettes.

PHIL: So I did.

He opens the packet, offers them to a couple of his mates.

PHIL: Church Hall. Chiswick. Not my cup of tea but she'd got a bee in her bonnet about it. Somebody'd hung up a couple of posters of Buenos Aires and left last year's Christmas lights up. About fifty people there. No obvious sex maniacs. Some nice-looking women but I think Vee's right. It's not about that. What it is about –

He gives a helpless shrug.

PHIL: It went on for ever.

VIRGINIA: *(To PHIL.)* They didn't rehearse any of this –

Eager to show him, she indicates other dancers.

VIRGINIA: – it's all improvised – he leads and she follows and somehow it all works. You see how fast their feet are moving? How quickly they change direction without agreeing it in advance? The thing she just did –

She indicates a step.

VIRGINIA: – that wasn't planned. She's probably never met him before tonight. They were complete strangers two minutes ago and now they're a couple. See that? And there? How do they do that?

PHIL: Not my cup of –

He sips from a mate gourd.

PHIL: – is this tea?

VIRGINIA: *Mate.* The Argentinians apparently drink it all day.

PHIL: Poor buggers.

He sets it down.

PHIL: We have to go.

VIRGINIA: *(To us.)* There was an Argentine couple on the floor, towards midnight. They were there to do an exhibition dance. I expected – *da-daa* –

She strikes one of the poses from the Tango that opened the show.

VIRGINIA: *(To PHIL.)* Coming –

She turns and turns back.

VIRGINIA: Wait –

PHIL: I thought we were – you know – *vrrmm vrrmm* –?

She becomes the overweight, elderly Argentine dancer ROSA.

VIRGINIA: *(To us.)* She was overweight. In a purple dress. Too much make-up. At least sixty or seventy years old. He was even older. I think he had some kind of heart thing, he took a handful of pills before he danced –

Rosa's elderly partner ALBERT pops pills and the bandoneon plays a slow Tango which they dance to as the elderly couple.

VIRGINIA: This wasn't one flashy step followed by another. It didn't seem to be about the steps at all. I didn't know what it was about but like everyone else there I couldn't take my eyes off them.

At one point she got too hot and –

She rests against a chair, panting, ungainly.

VIRGINIA: – she was just a very old lady panting for breath in a purple dress again – but when he took her back on the floor –

ALBERT: We dedicate this dance to our two beautiful daughters back home in Buenos Aires. We call them our twin Ferraris. And I dedicate myself to this woman – the most beautiful woman in the world, who I manufactured those Ferraris with.

VIRGINIA: – she *did* turn back into the most beautiful woman in the world.

PHIL: Sorry, love but –

He jingles his car keys.

PHIL: – early start tomorrow.

He takes a final look around, sums it up in a word.

PHIL: *Chiswick.*

VIRGINIA: One of my school teachers said to me *You mustn't expect too much from life, Virginia. I think that may be one of your problems, when you leave here.*

PHIL: Is that right?

VIRGINIA: This was the school which made me read *Anna Karenina* and *Jane Eyre* and *A Room Of One's Own.*

PHIL: Fancy that.

VIRGINIA: What did you make of tonight?

PHIL: I thought it was a bit sad.

VIRGINIA: Sad?

PHIL: How many times a week do they do that?

VIRGINIA: Some of them dance two or three times a week.

PHIL: If I ever got that lonely I'd say *Shoot me.*

VIRGINIA: If I said there's something about it that makes me realize that for the first time in my life I want something? *Want* it?

PHIL: Get in the car, Vins. You know what the A4's like even this time of night.

He turns to us.

PHIL: Next thing I know –

VIRGINIA picks up a backpack.

PHIL: You're going to walk out of your job and go to Buenos Aires? Just like that? Because that fat old woman and that skinny old guy –

VIRGINIA: This is about what happened when I started thinking about getting rid of all the filler we stuff our lives with, the same way painters have to cut and cut and cut before they can find what they really want to say.

PHIL: Hang on – I thought you weren't painting any more?

VIRGINIA: Figure of speech.

PHIL: Isn't that what life is made of? Habit? Filler? If that's what in the last resort it is?

VIRGINIA: Maybe it doesn't have to be.

PHIL: You're serious? South America? I mean –
South America?

She turns away from him, puts on the backpack.

VIRGINIA: *(To us.)* Packing is actually unpacking, isn't it? Sort of? Making decisions not just about what to leave behind but *who* you're leaving behind.

To her parents.

VIRGINIA: Bye, mum. Bye, dad. Bye, Phil.

A helpless shrug.

VIRGINIA: Bye, me.

She sits on a chair.

VIRGINIA: Heathrow. Six am. *What in God's name am I doing here?*

She sits on another chair.

VIRGINIA: Somewhere over the South Atlantic, six hours later. *Stop this plane. Turn it around. This is a terrible, terrible mistake.*

She sits on another chair.

VIRGINIA: Ezeiza Ministro Pistarini International Airport, Buenos Aires.

Elated, she savors the name of the city.

VIRGINIA: Buenos Aires.

She gets to her feet.

VIRGINIA: In the way in from the airport the taxi passed a small park, just a patch of grass, really, in the middle of the city; there was an elderly man in it by himself –

An ARGENTINE MAN sets down an old-fashioned boom box, switches it on and a scratchy old 78 RPM record of Fiorentino of the Anibal Troilo Orchestra singing 'Malena' plays. He moves to it; circling it slowly as if it's his partner; his body stiff with age but still responsive to the music.

VIRGINIA: – he didn't hear the traffic all around him or the hundreds of people criss-crossing the street – all that mattered was –

She listens to the music for a moment. When it ends the OLD MAN becomes the HOTEL OWNER who moves chairs and the table to create a hotel room, his English halting as he sets out a basin of water, towel and mirror.

HOTEL OWNER: English?

VIRGINIA: Yes.

HOTEL OWNER: You are Liverpool supporter?

VIRGINIA: No – I – don't really follow it.

HOTEL OWNER: You are to take Tango lessons here?

VIRGINIA: Yes.

HOTEL OWNER: You have chosen Tango school?

VIRGINIA: I thought I'd look around first.

He takes out a business card.

HOTEL OWNER: Best Tango School in Buenos Aires.
Two minutes away. Friend of mine. Marco. Great guy.
No rip off. Chinese restaurant on ground floor, you can't
miss it.

He rubs something off the card and hands it to her with a flourish.

HOTEL OWNER: Welcome to the most beautiful city in world,
where we think like Italians, speak Spanish and live as if
this is Paris –

She takes the card.

VIRGINIA: I didn't know it yet that they also call Buenos Aires
the Mecca of Lost Women but here I was.

She looks around the room.

VIRGINIA: A bed. A table. A light fitting that worked when it
chose. A bathroom with plumbing that talked to itself all
night long –

HOTEL OWNER: I phone him. He has room for one more
student. You are Man United fan, maybe?

He grimaces.

VIRGINIA: – I threw the window open and realized –

*We hear a cacophony of blaring traffic, squabbling in Spanish, a TV
playing a tele novella, competing radios playing different stations
and Tango playing from several bars at once –*

VIRGINIA: *I was here.*

She takes the backpack off.

VIRGINIA: Is this what my grandfather felt on the first night after his escape from Vienna? Exhilaration? Terror?

As if only now realizing it.

VIRGINIA: I know nobody here. I don't speak their language. There's no lock on the door.

She looks at the card.

VIRGINIA: How do I know I won't end up with my throat cut?

She looks in a mirror.

VIRGINIA: And who on earth is that?

But it's okay. You know – it's okay. In fact, it's great.

As she unpacks, PHIL phones.

PHIL: Hang on. You're not coming back any time soon; you're staying there for the time being; going to learn the Tango at a school you just heard about?

VIRGINIA: And it'll take at least six weeks.

PHIL: We are still engaged, are we?

VIRGINIA: Yes.

PHIL: The job?

VIRGINIA: I phoned them from Heathrow to explain.

PHIL: You know there's doing what you want to do in life, Virgers and doing what you *have* to do?

VIRGINIA: I need to start Tango all over again. Go right back to the first steps. The best – the only place in the world to do that is here.

PHIL: You know I like watches, Vi, don't you? Mechanical watches.

He takes his mechanical wrist watch off.

PHIL: They're amazing bits of engineering and artistry, how you fit a hundred and fifty bits and pieces together when some of the pieces are so small you can hardly see them. There are even some movements that account for the gravitational pull of the moon on the mainspring. Always been fascinated by them, I have. Took my granddad's pocket watch apart when I was eight or nine, there was hell to pay about that. Before I met you I seriously considered going to Switzerland to learn the trade. I was about to sign the indentures, book a flight. Backed out at the last minute. Saw sense. Took this job instead.

He starts to lose patience.

PHIL: That's what people do, Vinny. In the real world. They don't clear off and sign up for – they don't throw everything over on a – and aren't we supposed to be getting – you know – *ding dong, here comes the bride?* In the near future?

VIRGINIA: What if they're the same thing, Phil? Having to do something and wanting to do it? If you're not left any choice?

PHIL: It's a dance, that's all.

VIRGINIA: It's an art form. That's what I'm starting to realize. It's not about gesture – it's about truth.

PHIL: Art? We're going in for a mortgage.

He puts the phone down, turns to a disbelieving friend.

PHIL: Done a runner. Buenos Aires. It's not in Brazil, no, that's the other one. Her of all people. The Tango. Buenos Aires. That's what I said. The bloody Tango.

The bandoneon plays that same waterfall of notes she heard when she first heard Tango as VIRGINIA checks the address on the business card. MARCO is having a furious argument with someone offstage as she enters his studio –

MARCO: I stole your student? I did not steal your student. If somebody realizes they are wasting their money trying to learn bullshit tango from bullshit teacher and decide to come to my studio to learn from real teacher –

He turns to VIRGINIA.

MARCO: Yes? What?

He sees the business card.

MARCO: Come in –

He turns back to the argument.

MARCO: How is that stealing your student, you son of a –?

As VIRGINIA hesitates –

MARCO: I said come in.

He addresses the class.

MARCO: Good morning, my dear students. Welcome to the
*Ciudad de la Santísima Trinidad y Puerto de Santa María del
Buen Aire.* To six weeks of pain and suffering and perhaps,
at the very end, one perfect moment which will be gone
like that – *(Snaps his fingers.)* – but will stay with you for the
rest of your lives. Does anyone have any water?

VIRGINIA hands him a water bottle and he drinks it all down messily.

VIRGINIA: *(To us.)* Marco, in his scruffy shirt and tattoos, was
very definitely not in Pharmaceutical Sales, London and
the South East –

He snaps his fingers.

MARCO: You. In dress like nun with boring hair. Why are you
here?

VIRGINIA: I don't really know. It all happened so suddenly.
I went to a *milonga* by accident one week and weeks later I
walked out of my job and –

MARCO: That is not reason, no –

He throws the water bottle aside.

MARCO: It is because you have something in your head about
what Tango is; you see a bad movie some time, a show; the
sexy girl, the man whose eyes undress her; if this is what
you want please go –

He sits, folds his arms.

MARCO: – there are many places in Buenos Aires which will take
your money and teach you this. Go to them – you will go
back home and think you know this dance and people will –

He applauds sarcastically.

MARCO: – but you will have wasted your money because you
will have learned tricks, that is all –

He gets to his feet again.

MARCO: – clever tricks, yes – people will love them – but you can teach tricks to a monkey – people will clap for the monkey and give him banana –

He claps.

MARCO: – but the monkey knows it's just a trick and that he's a fake – that is why he has this sad little face – this sad little monkey face –

He mimes a monkey face.

MARCO: I do not want you going back to your real life with that monkey face – I want you to take piece of my country with you – piece of me – piece of Tango so we will begin at beginning. You will forget everything you think you know.

He indicates to the MUSICIAN who plays a simple series of notes.

MARCO: Tango begins with walk.

He indicates that VIRGINIA should walk, which she does, a little self-consciously.

MARCO: You are not here to learn to act Tango but to dance Tango, it is not about the steps, it is about soul.

When you dance Tango with someone you know them. If you dance any other dance you only know *about* them.

You are –?

VIRGINIA: Virginia.

MARCO: Virginia from –?

VIRGINIA: Buckinghamshire. England.

MARCO: *Good old Buckinghamshire* – where the women dress like nuns with boring hair.

VIRGINIA: What?

MARCO: The way you walk is more than disaster, by the way, is offense against God –

He puts his hand on her belly and she reacts.

MARCO: There is problem?

VIRGINIA: No.

MARCO: So walk. I lead. You follow.

He starts to walk, changing direction without warning, so that she has to follow by the touch of his hand as the music underscores.

MARCO: On window cill opposite my apartment lies a cat all day, in the sun. I watch it.

It strokes its whiskers, arches its back, pushes out a leg, shakes its head, stretches its claws out and I realize that is how cats dance. They move more slowly than we do in our dance but they have more time in the day than us and they fill it with dance. They are drunk on it. They do not care for anything else.

That is why a cat is happy to be by itself. It is working on its dance and when it sleeps it dreams its dance. That is why it has no speech. None that we understand.

Close your eyes.

She closes them, he keeps his hand on her and she follows.

MARCO: It does not care to speak because it is working on the true language of life which is a body moving in space and time and caring only that it be graceful; that is the one demand from the universe – that we use the bodies we have been loaned and blessed with to make beauty, by the grace of our limbs and our love of movement which is the love of life and the evidence that we possess it and to dance with partner is most special dance of all, is sacred thing because when I do this –

Open your eyes –

He opens his arms in the abrazo as she opens her eyes.

MARCO: – I expose my heart to you and when you step inside circle of my arms it is to say that you trust me, Virginia, that you know I will not hurt you –

She's about to move into his arms when he steps back.

MARCO: No. You are not ready. Not yet.

She moves away, pulls out a phone.

VIRGINIA: I'm in the dance studio with people from all over the world from ten until one –

As she talks she rehearses the elements that MARCO calls out, with a clap of his hands.

MARCO: *Ocho! Ocho! Ocho!*

VIRGINIA: *(Phone.)* – and then from three until six and every night and then we all go to a *milonga* somewhere –

MARCO: *Gancho! Gancho! Gancho!*

VIRGINIA: *(Phone.)* Am I happy? – I've been too busy to ask that but, mum, listen, it's super super important that you do something for me, there's something I need you to send me today –

MARCO: Caress the floor with your foot; caress me with your leg – not like that – not flapping around like dying fish on slab –

VIRGINIA: *(Phone.)* Not tomorrow, okay, today –

MARCO: Why are you looking at your feet? What is so interesting down there? Did you step in something on the street?

VIRGINIA: *(Phone.)* It's really important –

MARCO: Your thigh must wrap around mine – you know where your thigh is? – you have heard of it? – you have one –? Good. *Bueno.* Yes. With power, now. Not so tense but with power. Yes.

Do it again –

VIRGINIA: *(To us.)* I'd wanted the real thing. Was this it?

MARCO: Your foot must step into the place where mine is. Do not go around it. Go into it. Without fear. No apologies or second thoughts. It is your space now, English. Take it.

VIRGINIA: *(To us.)* And if it was, did I really want it?

MARCO: Glide like swan. Not bounce like duck. You are jumping up and down. Where is trampoline? Why do you do this?

VIRGINIA: *(To us.)* Or was I really here just to learn the tricks?

MARCO: You are always moving. Stop moving. Be still. Better, but don't stop dancing. No, you are moving again. Stop moving. Okay but don't stop dancing. Wait. *Wait.* You understand this word? You know what I mean when I say stop moving but keep dancing? When I go to *milonga* and

see beautiful dancer I do not say *See how she moves* I say
See how she waits.

He pulls her close.

MARCO: Your heart is beating faster, I think. It is not quite so
cold.

Good. *Good.* Interesting. There is something there,
perhaps. Who knows?

VIRGINIA: *(To us.)* Two people dropped out almost at once.
More left as it went on. This was hard. The hardest thing
I'd ever done. I somehow hung on, even when I was
in tears from the blisters on my feet and Marco had a
hangover –

She's now performing more complicated steps with MARCO.

MARCO: Oh my God, English, please, not like that. You are
bouncing again. Into my space, please. Without fear. Wrap
that leg around me. Don't you understand how to stop
moving but keep dancing?

What are you wearing? Are you Bride of Christ? Why is
your hair like that? Your hair is horrible. Is that a style or
do you just fall out of bed and leave it like that? Put it up.
I cannot have student with hair like that.

As she gathers her hair.

MARCO: You see Mr. Bandoneon there?

He indicates the MUSICIAN.

MARCO: He makes this beautiful music and you dance like it
is Oom-paah band in Bier Keller. If you don't want to learn
there is the door, goodbye, you waste my time.

She walks angrily towards the exit.

MARCO: Where are you going?

VIRGINIA: Maybe I'm wasting my time, too.

MARCO: So you run away – *boo-hoo* – like little girl?

VIRGINIA: I'm giving this everything. *Everything.* What more
do you want from me?

MARCO: To be the dancer you came here to be because unless you do that – listen to me – be the dancer you came here to be because if you do not do that you will never be the woman you are meant to be.

VIRGINIA: That probably sounds better in Spanish but does it mean anything?

She forces herself to go back to him to continue the steps.

MARCO: I respect you by learning your boring language. Why do you not do same, in my country?

VIRGINIA: I should do that, yes I know but I'm so tired every night – the class – then a *milonga* or a Tango club or a bar –

MARCO: There. All the time you complain. Your back hurts. Your stomach is upset. You need new dance shoes. You cannot get used to Argentine food. *Mate* gives you headache.

There is no air conditioning in the studio. You are tired all the time because you cannot sleep in that hotel.

VIRGINIA: I can't afford anywhere better.

MARCO: I have solution.

A lift.

MARCO: You bring your things to studio tomorrow and come home with me tomorrow night. You move in with Marco, we sleep together and I make sure you get here on time.

He sets her down.

VIRGINIA: I do what?

MARCO: Lift was not so bad, by the way. Not so good but not so bad.

VIRGINIA: Sleep with you?

MARCO: It is a very small apartment. Kitchen. Bedroom. How else do we make this work? To ask you to sleep on floor? It is impossible to ask this of you. We must share bed.

VIRGINIA: Do what?

MARCO: Also, I think I have dress for you. Dress to dance Tango in. Your size.

VIRGINIA: Share the bed?

MARCO: Yes and I think to say you will help with the meals and the expenses for the hot water and the electricity would be fair, yes? It is decided? This is what we will do?

Before she can respond.

MARCO: *Bueno.* Good.

A hesitation and then she picks up the backpack as if reluctant to shoulder it again as on the soundtrack we hear a noisy street with honking traffic and a radio playing a loud, impassioned football commentary.

VIRGINIA: *(To us.)* The flat was even smaller and less comfortable and in an even worse part of town than my hotel and God knows how many new students like me had moved in and Yes, I'm pretty sure the dress was left by another student – this dress –

She sets the backpack down and tugs at the almost prim, high-necked dress she's been wearing from the top of the show to reveal a simple, startlingly yellow dress underneath it. It's open at the neck and on her neck is a scar.

MARCO: That thing on your throat. That scar, Virginia. Is scar, yes? Tell me about scar.

VIRGINIA: It's not important.

MARCO: I will say if that is case. It is very noticeable.

VIRGINIA: Don't.

Her hands are covering it.

MARCO: Put your hands down.

She does so.

MARCO: My God. Jealous boyfriend? He tries to cut your throat when you say you leave him?

VIRGINIA: No. Yes. That's exactly what it was. No. That kind of thing doesn't happen in Buckinghamshire.

MARCO: So what happens? You try to kill yourself? Rope? Knife? How?

A projection shows an oddly beautiful, graphic, medical textbook image of a dissected thyroid. She speaks to us in the flat, lecturing way she did about the Bacon triptych.

VIRGINIA: The thyroid is composed of two lobes connected by an isthmus that lies on the trachea approximately at the level of the second tracheal ring. It is enveloped by the deep cervical fascia and is attached firmly to the trachea by the ligament of Berry. Each lobe resides in a bed between the trachea and larynx medially and the carotid sheath and sternocleidomastoid muscles laterally. An incision is made between two and four inches long –

Shaking her head, as if trying to understand what someone has just told her.

VIRGINIA: An incision? I'm sorry –?

He picks up a file and an X-ray as he becomes the DOCTOR.

DOCTOR: We don't really have any alternative with a cancer of the thyroid like this, I'm afraid. Surgery. As soon as we can clear a bed.

VIRGINIA: *(To us.)* One year before.

Look at his hands. See them? Butcher's hands. Not the delicate ones I imagined a surgeon would have. Like a – like a violinist or something. But of course they would have to be butcher's hands, wouldn't they? When you think about it.

DOCTOR: Gets a bit tricky sometimes in there – a millimeter or so either way and – it is possible that you could have some limited movement of your arms –

VIRGINIA: Limited –?

DOCTOR: I'll be working very near the vocal chords as well and sometimes – not often – I'll be as careful as I can, naturally – but in one percent of outcomes there's partial or total loss of speech.

VIRGINIA: I could lose my voice? For good?

DOCTOR: It's a very low percentage –

VIRGINIA: *(To us.)* Is that what he's saying? I don't understand. I wouldn't be able to speak again? Ever?

DOCTOR: In the overwhelming number of cases there are no adverse surgical outcomes –

VIRGINIA: But there are to the one percent and that has to be hundreds of people – thousands of people –

Fighting the distress.

VIRGINIA: I painted. I don't do it any more but – and not to have your voice – to not be able to –

DOCTOR: There really is no alternative, I'm sorry.

VIRGINIA: That's not – it isn't what –

DOCTOR: You should also know that I will leave a mark. You'll always have a reminder of what I have to do – and do as soon as possible.

VIRGINIA: I understand. *(To us.)* I didn't. Not really.

DOCTOR: Long term you'll be on medication. You're a –?

VIRGINIA: I'm sorry?

DOCTOR: What do you do for a living?

VIRGINIA: *(Her mind elsewhere.)* I – ah – I'm – I work in an auction house. Trainee.

DOCTOR: Not married?

VIRGINIA: Married? No. Engaged. Ish.

DOCTOR: No children?

VIRGINIA: No.

DOCTOR: Down the road there might be some issues – infertility – mood swings – weight problems – we'll talk you through those when the time's right –

VIRGINIA: I see. Yes. *(To us.)* I didn't.

PHIL: You understand what he's telling you, Virginia? You're following this?

VIRGINIA: Think so, Phil. Not sure. Need to – you know? Put thinking cap on.

She turns to PHIL, puzzled.

VIRGINIA: I kept looking at his hands –

PHIL: I'm sure he knows what he's doing, Vee.

VIRGINIA: The way he said it – *it gets a bit tricky in there sometimes* –

PHIL: You know what I'm saying, Vee? I'll be there.

VIRGINIA: If I can't speak? Or dress myself? If I can't have children? Put on so much weight that –

PHIL: I will be there. I will.

VIRGINIA: You don't know what you're promising. How could you? I'm not even sure what I heard.

PHIL: I mean it. I know things have been a bit rocky at times but I'm here. You're not getting rid of me. The thing in your –

He indicates his neck.

PHIL: – whatever it is – it isn't getting rid of me. Because I love you.

VIRGINIA: Thank you. I do love you, you know. I really do.

A heartfelt embrace and kiss and then she breaks away and turns back to us.

VIRGINIA: Bacon had it right. We are just meat.

The bandoneon underscores her with disjointed musical phrases which counterpoint the pain and panic in her words.

VIRGINIA: I asked for a mirror as soon as I came around from surgery but it was hard to see the face looking back at me as mine. There was something wrong with the eye and the flesh had been smeared as if someone had taken his thumb in wet oils and dragged it from my cheek to my chin. The ear looked as if it belonged to someone else; the chin had been taken off and put back on again, only not quite in the right place. Yet it was still a face. The way Bacon's faces are still faces, no matter what damage has been done to them, what horrors they have witnessed to turn them into horror. Was it the face of anyone I knew? Anyone I could ever get to know? *Was it still beautiful?*

Even more jagged, agitated phrases from the bandoneon complementing her mounting distress.

VIRGINIA: I put the mirror down so hard I nearly broke it but I had to pick it up again because Bacon wasn't finished with me yet. There was still the scar. The man who had painted me that morning hadn't been content to press his thumbs into my face and push it into another shape. He had stabbed me in the throat. Taken the spatula and dug it into the paint so violently the canvas had split; ripped me open and left me with my wound.

MARCO: This was big deal?

VIRGINIA: What?

MARCO: Big deal operation?

VIRGINIA: It was, yes. A really big deal.

MARCO: It is same word for cancer in Spanish. Interesting, yes? You are better now?

VIRGINIA: It's not one of the cancers that hangs around and hides and comes back years later but the medication – that's a lifetime thing.

MARCO: Mood swings? This means you act crazy?

VIRGINIA: Or I get depressed. Or my energy goes. I can't go without it for ten days or –

A shrug.

VIRGINIA: – you know.

MARCO: I don't.

VIRGINIA: It would be a real problem. I dropped my medicine down the toilet by accident a few days ago and had to get my mother to send me more.

MARCO: Or you would croak?

VIRGINIA: Croak?

MARCO: I hear this word in movies.

VIRGINIA: I would croak, yes.

MARCO: Yes is Yes – you must not be so English about this – not here.

VIRGINIA: *(Angry.)* Okay, yes, I've been told that if I ever stop taking my medication for ten days I would die. Why are you so interested in this?

MARCO: You are in my apartment. With big scar on neck.

VIRGINIA: *(Defensive.)* It's not so big, really.

MARCO: It is like – like *mariposa* – like butterfly.

VIRGINIA: That's what the shape of the thyroid is.

I have a boyfriend. Just so you know. A serious boyfriend. Fiancee, really.

MARCO: Who says he sticks with you whatever happens, like idiot –

VIRGINIA: He was being loyal and loving –

MARCO: Like I say, idiot, English idiot, all that rain gets in his brain.

VIRGINIA: It's not been a year since the operation and I'm in Buenos Aires – leaving him behind – doing something he doesn't understand –

MARCO: God Save the Queen. England Two, Argentina Four.

VIRGINIA: I love him. Don't think I don't.

MARCO: But you are here.

VIRGINIA: For the apartment. Because I'm running out of money.

MARCO: Let me think about scar.

VIRGINIA: You're going to throw me out because of it?

MARCO: Did I say that? You are very angry person, I think.

VIRGINIA: I'm not. Look, maybe I'd just better go. This was a mistake.

MARCO: I say you are most beautiful woman ever to walk through door of Tango school. Not just mine. Any Tango school in Buenos Aires. Any Tango school on planet.

VIRGINIA: Except for – which you couldn't help pointing at.

MARCO: Only because you hid it.

VIRGINIA: I didn't hide it. I did. I do. In England I did. I'm going. I'm not. Do you want me to stay?

MARCO: In Tango you cannot hide.

VIRGINIA: Oh God, I'm sick of hearing about Tango already, in some ways, how everything is Tango –

MARCO: In Tango is world. Tango explains everything.

A darker, more sinister Tango plays as MARCO moves towards her.

MARCO: There is another *milonga* you go to whether you like it or not, where you don't really want to be and you don't get choice whether to dance or sit this one out, *no gracias, not this time* –

He holds her in the abrazo as the music gets even darker, the lights even more ominous.

MARCO: You say *No, there is some mistake* but Death pulls you to your feet and takes you onto dance floor –

He starts to dance with her, her body unwilling to move but given no choice.

MARCO: It could have anyone but he chooses you; you try to resist him but you have no choice but to dance with him; you follow him because he's done this many times with many people, none of whom wanted him to hold them so close –

Her reluctance to dance with him shows in her movements but she's still on the floor, in his tight grip.

MARCO: You danced with him but with help of wonderful National Health Service – I have read about this – you got away for now with only huge ugly scar on neck but you know, Virginia from England, what most people do not know, what it is to do that dance and survive – to follow *El Muerte* step by step and not give in. To do that you found something strong in you that you did not know was there –

Now VIRGINIA is taking the lead in the dance, fighting back, refusing to give in.

MARCO: *Bravo*, Virginia. You stood up to the son of bitch, you beat him although we know you never really win, not in game like this but you get away, this time –

Then you hear Tango one day – one bar – one note, that is all it takes – and you know that Tango is also dance with Death and you come here to celebrate escape from him in most alive and I say, as *porteno*, most beautiful and therefore holy city in world –

Vere dignum et iustum est, aequum et salutàre, nos tibi sancte Pater –

– that is what brings you here – this is power of Tango – this is why I say in Tango is world, in Tango is explanation for everything – why I say I am Pope of Tango; perhaps even in some way, God of Tango, not just boring teacher in school in back street where I do not know from one month to next if I can afford to pay rent – this is why you are here in my apartment in that dress which makes you even more beautiful and which you will now take off carefully and come to bed –

Quickly, please. I have to teach tomorrow. Scar is no problem, I have made decision. But that really is good color for you, yes.

She hesitates, unsure whether to go ahead with this or not. From somewhere nearby a radio plays 'Malena'.

VIRGINIA: What is that song?

MARCO: It is famous Tango song *Malena*. A man sings about how when Malena sings the Tango he realizes the pain she must have suffered to have such a voice. To put such feeling into it.

VIRGINIA: It's beautiful.

MARCO: There is story that Homero Manzi wrote it about Elena Tortolero and when she heard it and realized it was about her she refused to sing it.

VIRGINIA: She didn't like what he wrote?

MARCO: It says how much of her heart she pours into her song, how her voice, like the bandoneon's, is full of pain – it talks of her eyes and lips and hands and veins and the scent that comes from her – how she gives the song everything – and he is, I believe, talking not about her singing but how she makes love, how abandoned she is in bed – a woman who will give everything for pleasure, even though it drags her through the mud.

VIRGINIA: Oh.

MARCO: This should have been private thing, between her and man she shared bed with. You are woman, you will agree with this, I think. You understand even more than men that Desire without Technique is only Appetite and what men and women do together in the little space of time we have before we all go into the darkness – my beautiful Virginia, my perhaps soon-to-be lover – what we may do in that bed tonight is with your consent – that you enter the *abrazo* of your own free will – and I promise on my life that I will never betray your trust – that if you give me the gift of your nakedness I will not share it with the world – not even to celebrate the body and the soul and the heart of the most beautiful and complete woman I have ever known.

He opens his arms in an abrazo. She turns to us, ruefully.

VIRGINIA: It's safe to say – it's safe to say I'm not in Buckinghamshire any more.

She doesn't commit herself yet as 'Malena' plays on; the MUSICIAN adding live bandoneon to the arrangement as the lights fade.

End of Act One.

Act Two

At the piano, the MUSICIAN starts one tango piece, stops, play some bars of another, goes back to the first, improvises on that one, stops playing for a moment, 'thinks' about what to play next and then stops halfway through the piece he's decided to play.

VIRGINIA enters, towelling her hair dry. She's learned some of the Spanish words of 'Malena', sings/hums them to herself –

VIRGINIA: *(Sings.) Malena canta el tango como ninguna*
Y en cada verso pone su corazón,
A yuyo de suburbio su voz perfuma,
Malena tiene pena de bandoneón.

Making love without having to make arrangements – I'd never lived with anyone before – this was new.

She sings/hums the tune again.

VIRGINIA: *Tal vez allá, en la infancia, su voz de alondra*
Tomó ese tono oscuro de callejón,
O acaso aquel romance que sólo nombra
Cuando se pone triste con el alcohol –

I can't pretend that Marco wasn't a bit of a brute – that was also part of his charm but charm is also a kind of bullying; a means of getting your own way and though he made me feel more alive than any man had ever done I couldn't help but think of something Goethe wrote that where there is much light there is much shadow. More and more though, I was beginning to think that's where the interesting stuff is.

We hear a Buenos Aires traffic report on the radio. She hears a word and she opens a phrase book to check on it.

VIRGINIA: *Importantes obras viales* – major road works.

She writes it down in small notebook.

VIRGINIA: I wake at five with Marco's tattooed arm across me and think *It is possible to have both Wisdom and Serenity. The body's Wisdom that I find on the dance floor and in bed with this man. The Serenity of the spirit that comes from knowing I am in the place the Universe means me to be in, in this moment.*

His breath is sour with the *Quilmes* and *Fernet Branca* and *Vino Tinto* he drank last night and he hasn't shaved for several days. *Tener un afeitado.* To shave. He likes to sleep late so I ease out from underneath that arm and sit on the side of the bed for a moment, wondering which part of me hurts most today.

There's a patch of sunlight on the floor that looks like a pool of fire. I step into it. A cockroach runs to safety under the stove. They hardly bother me now, although my feet are bare. *La cucaracha.* The cockroach.

She sings/hums the refrain.

VIRGINIA: *(Sings.) Malena canta el tango con voz de sombra, Malena tiene pena de bandoneón.*
I stand at the window for a moment. The English painter, Lowry, once said –

She stops, as if puzzled, momentarily about why she uses so many quotes.

VIRGINIA: Quotes – all those quotes – in my head – as if I'm not really allowed to think it unless –

She shakes her head as if to clear it of all those quotes.

VIRGINIA: No more quotes. Not here. Not with him. In this new life. The new me. Whose back hurts, whose ankles are swollen, who's beginning to think there's something seriously wrong with her hip but is going to ignore it, as she ignores the headache and the faint feeling of nausea that's always there.

We hear a Buenos Aires weather report on the radio as she checks the phrase book again.

VIRGINIA: *Con una probabilidad de lluvias.* With a chance of showers.

Today, like every day, I will dance for six hours at the studio and tonight go by myself or with some of the other students to a *milonga.* Today, like every day, I will find a reason not to phone or e-mail Phil and my parents much more than a few words, although sometimes I will write about what I have seen that day.

Her, for example –

On the screen we see several images of street art containing an image of a naked woman with flaming red hair.

VIRGINIA: I begin to notice her everywhere; through a bus window, sitting on the back of Marco's motorbike. No helmet, of course. A vision of the ideal woman, forever out of reach? As perfection in the Tango is always this far of reach –? *(Indicates.)* One night I found her on a wall down an alley in the Boca –

Electro Tango sounds.

VIRGINIA: – I found myself in one of the Queer Tango Clubs I'd heard about –

She sits, uncomfortable and feeling out of place. A hesitant nod to the invisible partner who asks her to dance and she gets to her feet. At first she's a little stiff and awkward; then relaxes into it; then discovers that Queer Tango allows you to experiment with gender and role. Finally she throws English, suburban caution to the winds and gives herself totally to her feelings. At the end she's breathless and surprised at how much she's opened herself up.

VIRGINIA: She kissed me. I kissed her back.

ERIK: You look different. Your eyes are shining.

VIRGINIA: *(To us.)* This was Erik. Another student. He told us he'd been a drunk for twenty years. He'd been about to throw himself off a bridge when he decided to learn Tango instead. There were a lot of stories like that in the studio.

ERIK: Did something happen to you?

VIRGINIA: *(To us.)* I hadn't really noticed him. There was so much to learn, the days were so busy.

To ERIK.

VIRGINIA: I'm thinking of staying on. In Buenos Aires. Getting a job in a bar – maybe walking people's dogs in the Recoleta –

A beat.

VIRGINIA: You know what? Until I said that I'd no idea I was even thinking of it. But now I've said it – that is what I'm going to do.

ERIK: That first day when you walk into studio with ugliest backpack I have ever seen – you are late and look scared and tired – I remember this moment when I first see you –

He angles one hand.

ERIK: You are here and light is there –

He angles another hand.

ERIK: I am here and I watch you for moment before you turn around and in that moment I know. I *know. This is why I have come here. This is what all my life has been leading to.* I know that when you turn and see me this is what you will know, too but you have eyes only for Marco, like rest of women in that room but he is wrong for you, I know this; I do not want you to be hurt the way you are going to be hurt when these six weeks are over.

VIRGINIA: *(As gently as she can.)* Is that really any of your business?

ERIK: Truth is, he is not greatest Tango teacher. Why have so many people left? Yes, he has great line in Argentine bullshit, Tango bullshit but he is not even that good a dancer. He was worker in automobile plant in Pachecho – bandoneon player tells me this –

He turns to the MUSICIAN.

ERIK: This is correct? *(Back to VIRGINIA.)* Volkswagen factory – he hangs out in Tango clubs and bars dancing with tourists – he gives private lessons – you understand? – private lessons, you can guess what that means –

VIRGINIA: I'm not comfortable having this conversation –

She tries to move away but he stays with her.

ERIK: Look at students from other schools – they are learning better than we are here in lousy room above terrible Chinese restaurant without air conditioning.

VIRGINIA: So why did you stay?

ERIK: Because of you. It's not possible you do not know this.

VIRGINIA: I'm sorry but –

Again she tries to move away and again he follows.

ERIK: That dress you are wearing – he gave you this dress, yes? Ask the bandoneon player if he saw this dress before.

He turns to the MUSICIAN.

ERIK: Tell her what you told me. At least two girls wear this dress. Tell her –

The MUSICIAN holds up three fingers, then a fourth.

ERIK: See? He sits at back of the room and does not say much but he sees everything.

The hours we have spent together here – the times we have danced together – you must know. How could you not know? We have been this close together for five weeks –

VIRGINIA: *(To us.)* There was a little too much shadow to Erik but maybe the danger of this was what I wanted, too. No going back. I'd jumped off a cliff and you can't decide to stop halfway down –

The bandoneon strikes a sudden, harsh, startling series of chords and we go into an apache dance to Tango music; a piece of theatrical dance drawn from the following elements.

Night in the dangerous dockland on the edge of the city. It's been so hot during that day that even at midnight the shadows seem to smoke. Overhead the gantries of the huge cranes tower in silhouette. The rats scuttle underfoot and somewhere in the darkness there's a gunshot. He comes here every night to search, ever since he caught a momentary glimpse of her through the train window as it flashed by. In that moment she'd looked up at him as if she knew what he knew, instantly. That neither of their lives could be completed until they were together. So he slips a knife into his sleeve, because here where the outcasts live you might have to fight for your life, and he follows the twists and turns of the narrow streets, searching for her.

He knows she's somewhere here looking for him, too. Looking in the Tango bars and the dance halls. Looking in the cafes and the clubs. Taking her life in her hands, too (With maybe a pearl-handled .22 in her purse to even the odds.) in order to complete the circle of their lives.

On the hottest night of the hottest day of the year, when the water in the river bubbles like tar and even the concrete sweats, he finds her. Her head is lowered, she looks sad and thoughtful and he knows it's because she hoped this night would bring him to her and her long nights of searching would be over, too. Then she brushes a stray lock of hair back from her forehead and looks up pensively and a smile lights her face. There's a bead of perspiration on her upper lip and her cheeks suddenly flush and she's risen from the yellow chair she's been sitting in and walks past him to embrace the man who entered behind him.

It's a mistake. Of course it's a mistake. Or she's teasing him. Or there's a reason she has to pretend to be with this stranger who is leaving the bar with her on his arm. She'll turn at the door and smile at him and he'll know that she knows that it's him she's been searching for; him who has finally come to her. Then why does she tuck her hand so tightly under the stranger's arm and bury her head in his shoulder for a moment? Why does she step into the street without a backward glance? Why does she throw her head back and laugh at something the stranger has just said to her and allow him to draw her to him? She must know she's with the wrong man. How could she not?

The knife has slid into his hand, as if it's got a life of its own. The stiletto can put this right. One quick thrust, just below the shoulder blade, straight into the heart. Even before the body has hit the ground she'll be in his arms, having come to her senses. She'll blink and say 'Thank God' or 'Why did you wait so long?' or 'I was afraid you'd let him take me from you'. Then she'll do that already achingly familiar thing with that lock of hair and touch his lips and everything will be all right. It'll be all right for ever. Nothing will ever be bad again for either of them. All it will take is one swift and – really – painless strike.

He grips the knife tightly, making sure not to lodge his thumb under his finger because that's how to break it when you stab a man. He's behind them in the street, closing fast. Three more steps, two more, one more step and then he'll act. Hearing his footsteps the couple stop, turn, look at him, puzzled. Her eyes say 'Do I know you?' and he realizes in that moment that she has no idea who he is. That he's the stranger to her and always will be and for one moment the realization makes him want to use the knife on her, instead. To send that blade flashing at her and then turn it on himself, with her blood still on it.

He doesn't. The knife slips back into his sleeve and he mumbles some excuse and turns away, stumbling on the curb. Then he turns again and watches as they walk on, along that narrow harbor street, under the huge shapes of the cranes, lost in each other, him already forgotten. Overhead the red neon sign of a Tango bar pulses like the blood in his heart…

PHIL: Is she all right, do you think? Only she's been sending me –

On the screen we see the images of the naked red-haired woman, painted by the street artist.

PHIL: Nowt wrong with it, of course – art, I suppose, she's always been big on that – but –

He hesitates.

PHIL: They took my own mum away once, when I was a kid. She got into this thing where she'd start crying as soon as she got up in the morning, couldn't stop. It was horrible. One time a bloke in the office disappeared. Turned up six months later in Brighton with the Krishnas.

So when she takes off like that – and this –

He indicates the images.

PHIL: I'm not saying it's – but if there's anything I should know –

He listens.

PHIL: That's grand. That's a great relief. I had to ask –

He listens.

PHIL: I'm sure you're right. That's probably it. She works so hard at her job and with the wedding coming up –

He listens.

PHIL: That's what it'll have been. A little holiday. I'm glad we cleared the air.

He turns to his friends, offering his cigarettes again.

PHIL: What could I say to them? Your precious darling Virginia is acting like a spoiled brat? It's not how grown-ups behave? It makes me – and them – look like bloody fools?

He listens.

PHIL: Look on the bright side? There's only a week to go? She'll have got it out of her system? I suppose – let's hope –

He looks up at the images of the naked red-headed woman.

PHIL: I'm not an idiot because I don't get that, am I? I've got a right to say if you call that Art, if you call dancing the Tango, *Art* –

He gives up, shrugs, puts the cigarettes away, takes out his phone.

PHIL: Meet you at Heathrow, shall I, then, Vinners? No? You're sure? Christ, I have missed you. I think I've found a house, by the way. Needs a bit of work but it could be just the job.

On the screen appears a photo of a small, boxy, suburban house with a scrap of garden. Under it is the legend JUST THE JOB.

PHIL: You're absolutely sure? Hang on. Give me the flight number again, in case you change your mind –

VIRGINIA: *(To us.)* I'd missed him, too, in an odd way. Just couldn't do the thing with the flowers and the balloon at Heathrow. *(To PHIL.)* Honest. No. It's okay. I'd rather just find my own way, thanks. *(To us.)* I could – I should – have told him there and then about Marco and staying on but for a moment there my heart had become the cold, small, careful, English one again and the chance was gone.

Then I looked at *Just the Job* and I could see the pansies and petunias and the crazy paving in the garden and the bench from the Garden Centre and I tried to imagine myself there in five years time with, I suppose, my children if the medication hasn't scuppered that but I didn't want *Just the Job* children, I wanted Marco's children, shouting in Spanish, racing up and down the stairs of an apartment somewhere in Buenos Aires, the kind of place mum and dad would be horrified to think I was living, messy and noisy and the neighbors calling across the balconies to one another and radios and TVs playing too loud and instead of a night out being *Just the Job* in a pub it would be a *milonga* together, me and the man I loved and maybe with another child on the way because he'd take me when he wanted and I had learned to hold nothing back, either –

With a desperate urgency she pulls out the phone.

VIRGINIA: Phil. Phil. Pick up. Please pick up. I have to tell you something –

MARCO: I have question for you, my Virginia.

She puts the phone away.

MARCO: You have heard of Garganta del Diablo?
It is waterfall in Iguazu National Park; most amazing waterfall in world.

VIRGINIA: Is that the question?

MARCO: What question? Oh yes. Question later. Garganta de Diabolo. You have worked hard, my Virginia. Before you leave you deserve to see world famous tourist site. Only one hour away from Buenos Aires but different side of my country –

A deep thunderous sound wells up; reverberating until it shakes the walls; the unleashed power of the tumbling water making her stare outwards and upwards, as if in wonder at the falls.

On the screen is a violent swirl of white water; pooling and eddying with savage force. MARCO has to shout above the sound.

MARCO: You have heard of The Disappeared? The Mothers of the Plaza de Mayo who stand there for years wanting to know what the military did to their sons and daughters? The students who were tortured and killed; the pregnant women whose babies were taken away from them after they were shot? The revolutions. The assassinations. You wake up one day and they tell you all the money you had in the bank is gone – *ppfffff* –

He gestures.

MARCO: That is my country, too. Like this is.

The sound rises to a crescendo and then fades.

VIRGINIA: The question?

MARCO: Question?

VIRGINIA: Something you brought me here to ask me?

MARCO: Ah yes.

You are from Buckinghamshire, yes?

VIRGINIA: Yes.

MARCO: Queen of England lives in Buckingham Palace?

VIRGINIA: Yes.

MARCO: Same Buckingham?

VIRGINIA: Yes.

MARCO: But palace is in London? Not Buckinghamshire?

VIRGINIA: Is that – is that what you wanted to ask me?

MARCO: It comes up in conversation.

VIRGINIA: This doesn't have to be my last weekend here, Marco. In fact, I've decided that it's not.

MARCO: You pay for six weeks. Six weeks is nearly over, goodbye.

VIRGINIA: It's time for me to say that I love you and for you to manage to get out the words that you love me.

She kisses him.

VIRGINIA: There. Say it.

MARCO: This thing you say – about not going back –

VIRGINIA: I'm going to stay in Buenos Aires with you because there are moments when I'm dancing when I'm in touch with something that I've been looking for all my life. I am more complete, in those moments, than I have ever been and I want to find a way to join those moments together; to live in a circle of completed moments of fulfillment which you have helped me get to.

MARCO: In Spanish, please.

VIRGINIA: I'm learning to speak Tango, that's all I can take in for now and at some point the Spanish will come.

MARCO: Is beautiful language but how will you live?

VIRGINIA: I'll find something. Work in a bar, anything.

MARCO: Where will you live?

VIRGINIA: In the apartment with you.

MARCO: Is small apartment.

VIRGINIA: Maybe we'll find somewhere else. If we ever have a baby we'll need that anyway.

MARCO: You are going to have baby?

VIRGINIA: No but if we do.

MARCO: Virginia – please – I am Tango teacher. I teach The Tango. That is all I do. These other things – circles of whatever they are – I do not know about.

VIRGINIA: In Tango is world. Tango explains everything. You said that. You're the Pope of Tango, maybe the God of Tango, remember?

MARCO: To a point.

VIRGINIA: You didn't just teach me a dance. You taught me not to hide. About anything.

MARCO: I agree to teach you Tango. Now you want to live rest of life with me?

VIRGINIA: *(Stung.)* I get six weeks, a crash course in Argentine cooking, the speech about the cat and don't forget to hand the Tango dress back for the next student? Nothing else?

MARCO: I work in Volkswagen factory in Pachecho before I open dance studio.

VIRGINIA: I know.

MARCO: You do?

VIRGINIA: I know about the private lessons and how many students wore this dress before me.

MARCO turns to the MUSICIAN.

MARCO: I will speak with you afterwards, Mr. Bandoneon.

Back to VIRGINIA.

MARCO: Believe me, this is better than working in automobile factory but is business, too.

VIRGINIA: You know what this adds up to, you and me. You must do.

MARCO: The *abrazo* –

He holds her in an abrazo.

MARCO: The embrace of equals. Two people who will dance together but will be responsible for themselves. I lead. You choose to follow or not. Woman is not victim, here. She is in charge of own body.

Please, this is not a good thing you are doing, to make plans for other person's life. I told you. I worked in automobile factory. You know what that is like?

VIRGINIA: I don't. No. I can guess.

MARCO: You can?

VIRGINIA: I can't. No. Okay? I'll try. I will – but all that Spanish you spoke in bed, all the things you whispered to me that I didn't understand –

MARCO: I think Virginia is very special person but – excuse me – maybe this – this butterfly that landed on her neck –

He indicates the scar.

MARCO: – makes Virginia think she deserves something different because of what happened to her. She says *Is not enough to learn Tango from this man, I must go to bed with him –*

VIRGINIA: *(Bewildered.)* That is not how it happened –

MARCO: Marco speaks. You will get on plane on day it says on ticket. You will go back to London. You will go back to your job as painter –

VIRGINIA: I'm not a painter, didn't you listen to anything I ever said? I worked in an auction house.

MARCO: Is simple story, this story. Buenos Aires story. Girl – woman – comes here to dance Tango and sleep with Tango teacher.

VIRGINIA: Fall in love with.

MARCO: Same story.

VIRGINIA: No.

MARCO: Yes. No. Maybe. Sleep with teacher and then go home. God save the Queen. Argentina four, England nil. But does student ever ask what teacher wants? Teacher who is trying to pay rent on studio; stop other *puto* teachers stealing his students; pay for two kids to go to school in nice clothes and not in rags –

VIRGINIA: Two –?

MARCO: Valentina and Julieta –

VIRGINIA: Your –?

MARCO: My two little girls, yes – different mothers but – you want to see a photo, no? Every tango teacher is same thing. Is hazard of profession.

VIRGINIA: But if you're not with their mothers –

MARCO: My daughters stay with me, sometimes. In city. I take care of them in vacation times. I promise I will have no one here then.

VIRGINIA: I won't make it a problem –

MARCO: Real life, Virginia. We are talking about real life now. Not bloody Tango school romance.

VIRGINIA: That is not what this is.

MARCO: What else – pardon me – can it be?

VIRGINIA: This is real. What we have here. It's nothing to do with the studio.

MARCO: It is all about studio. When door is open and new students arrive do you know what Marco is looking for?

VIRGINIA: No I don't, Marco – what is that?

MARCO: American heiress from Dallas.

VIRGINIA: What?

MARCO: I don't even say beautiful heiress. Need not even be Dallas. Or American. I say woman who will insist *Come with me to Texas.* Or Chicago. Or Miami. I want big house. Boat. Never to have to work again. Never to teach bloody Tango again. *Ocho. Ocho. Gancho. Ocho.*

VIRGINIA: That's – no – that can't be it –

MARCO: But if it is what Marco wants?

VIRGINIA: It's not, no, no, it's not –

MARCO: Whatever you look for, answer is not me. Tango in the end is only a dance and Buenos Aires is only big, uncomfortable city, not centre of universe.

VIRGINIA: It isn't just a dance and Buenos Aires is the centre of the Tango universe and I have to stay and if you won't let me stay with you because you care nothing for me I'll find somewhere else.

MARCO: You have no money left. No permit to work.
No place to stay – but you can keep the dress. I will always have happy memory of time we had together in my apartment and I still say you are most beautiful woman ever to walk through door.

VIRGINIA: So then, Marco? So *then*?

MARCO: For me, it is all about the *abrazo*. The embrace.
That first moment when you hold a new person so close. Everything then is possible. All doors are open. One by one they will close. But that first moment, as the music begins –

The bandoneon plays the first chords of Tango she ever heard; the one that started her journey.

MARCO: We dance together one last time and then make love one last time, on edge of waterfall.

VIRGINIA: Oh God – you don't have a speech about making love on the edge of a waterfall too, do you?

MARCO: No but it is important to live with style.

They dance to a Tango played on the violin, in an echo of how the old couple danced together. Several times he tries to pull away, indicating that the dance is over and so is their relationship.

Panicked, heart-broken, she refuses to let him go and uses elements of his teaching to try to persuade him to stay – placing his hand on her belly and clutching it tightly, forcing him to follow her as she first followed him.

VIRGINIA: Close your eyes –

She holds his hand there with both of her hands. He tries to pull them free but she's desperate to keep him. MARCO's had enough, turns to the MUSICIAN.

MARCO: Mr. Bandoneon!

The MUSICIAN stops playing halfway through a phrase which hangs in the air. MARCO turns away and the MUSICIAN picks up his music sheets and exits, leaving the stage entirely.

VIRGINIA picks up the backpack.

VIRGINIA: On the way to the airport I asked the taxi driver to stop by that small park where I'd seen the old man working on his steps by himself. He wasn't there.

She sits on a chair.

VIRGINIA: Ezeiza Ministro Pistarini International Airport, Buenos Aires. Ten a.m.

I'll look up and MARCO will be there to ask me to come back.

Nope.

She moves to another chair.

VIRGINIA: Three that afternoon, somewhere over the South Atlantic.

Stop this plane. Turn it around. Was it only six weeks ago that I was headed in the other direction?

She moves to another chair.

VIRGINIA: At one point on the flight back they asked for the window shades to be pulled down for those who wanted to sleep or watch a movie. We were flying into daylight. I'd been sunk in misery the entire flight but when I heard that phrase I thought *Maybe I am flying into daylight. Maybe these weeks will have changed everything; made everything clearer.* But there was the same grey cloud over Heathrow that had been there when I left. The same rain streaming down the windows.

NEIL: Can I help you with that, love?

VIRGINIA: Sure, dad.

NEIL: Your room is just like you left it.

VIRGINIA: Magic.

NEIL: Did you have a good time?

VIRGINIA: Sort of.

NEIL: Got it out of your system?

VIRGINIA: *(To us.) Home is so sad.*
  It stays as it was left,

Shaped to the comfort of the last to go
As if to win them back.

Larkin must have been thinking of my room when he wrote that. *(Bleakly.)* I'm quoting again. I've hardly got back and I'm using other people's words instead of my own.

NEIL: You want to talk about it?

VIRGINIA: Not just yet. A lot happened.

NEIL: Good things? Mainly?

VIRGINIA: I don't know. Not right now.

NEIL: I don't know if I get it, Virginia. Or your mum. I don't know that we ever will. We're just glad to have you back in one piece. I know Phil will be, too –

He hugs her and then becomes PHIL.

PHIL: Crisps?

VIRGINIA: What?

PHIL: Packet of crisps? I don't think there's food in this pub this time of night.

He holds out a packet of crisps.

VIRGINIA: No crisps, thanks. One of the reasons I didn't really stay in touch was because I was living with my Tango instructor.

PHIL: I thought there might be something dodgy going on.

VIRGINIA: It's over now.

PHIL: Sure?

VIRGINIA: By the width of the Atlantic, yes. *(To us.)* Although I still halfway hoped I'd look up to see Marco standing at the bar.

PHIL: I appreciate you telling me that, Virginia and I need to level with you about a couple of things as well –

VIRGINIA: *(To us.)* – which were a girl from the office and a girl at a party and the wife of his best friend.

PHIL: Whew. Glad I got that off my chest. I thought I'd put everything out there.

VIRGINIA: That thing you told me about watches – you've never thought maybe you should do it, after all?

PHIL: Too late now.

VIRGINIA: Is it? Really?

PHIL: I'm in line for Regional Manager –

VIRGINIA: The way you talked about it – the whatever-it-was the moon affects – even down the phone I could tell –

PHIL: It's done. I don't regret it.

VIRGINIA: You must do.

PHIL: I'm not from your world, Vee, where you can walk out of a job just like that –

VIRGINIA: There was every sort of person in that Tango school –

PHIL: I said it's done.

VIRGINIA: Everybody was broke or just getting by – you don't need to be from *my world* to follow your passion.

PHIL: Done.

VIRGINIA: It might even be harder, being middle class – you're not expected to be really serious about anything –

PHIL: *Done.*

VIRGINIA: *(Insistent.)* I'd stick with you, the way you stuck with me after the operation.

PHIL: I did that because I love you. And you love me, right?

VIRGINIA: I do, yes –

PHIL: So that's all right then, isn't it? Put the flags out. We're back on again.

VIRGINIA: Back on?

PHIL: The wedding? The house?

VIRGINIA: The Just the Job, house?

BARMAN: Time, ladies and gents!

PHIL: The what?

VIRGINIA: I'm giving you all of me. I want to have all of you. If there's a bit of you that wants to be somewhere else –

BARMAN: Now then, boys and girls, we've all got homes to go to!

VIRGINIA: If there's still a chance you could do it – the watch-making –

PHIL: Don't start that again.

BARMAN: Glasses, please!

PHIL: Is that right then, Vee? What you just said? I have all of you? From now on?

VIRGINIA: *(To us.)* We went back to his place and made love. How was it? After Marco? Tea and biscuits. I'd be settling for that, now.

NEIL: Is it good news, Virginia? Can I tell your mum it's back on?

VIRGINIA: I think it is, dad. Back on. It is good news, yes. Put the flags out. It is great to have it all sorted out. Just the Job.

> *VIRGINIA pulls on the original high-necked dress as she speaks with a visual fragment of one of Bacon's intimidating images on the wall behind her.*

VIRGINIA: The suicide, in Bacon's own hotel room, of his long-time friend and lover, George Dyer, led to the most compelling of the triptychs. The unblinking yet anguished eye of the artist spares himself, the subject and us none of the horror of the moments before, during and after the death of someone every inch of whose body he had known, as the other had known every inch of his.

A *die-er* – painted by a *Bacon*.

Look.

To possess is to be possessed. To demand the use of the beloved's body for one's own pleasure is to surrender our own body for them to use, for their pleasure; our love for them – theirs for us – must be based, Bacon tells us, in a frank acceptance of our carnal natures – carnal as in sexual, carnal as in carnivorous – a feasting of the flesh which ends in death or the end of an affair; which, so often, can feel like the end of everything that matters, in that part of our soul has been torn from us – the soul that his searching brush looks for in vain on the canvas but in life, if we are lucky, we may find, once in a while, beating in time with that of another creature like ourself.

BLENNERHASSET: Good God.

VIRGINIA: Mr. Blennerhasset?

BLENNERHASSET: Belly.

VIRGINIA: *(To us.)* I think the general opinion at work and at home was that I had had some kind of breakdown. Delayed shock. Major wobbler. It must have finally caught up with me that I was being told that I could die. But it was all going to be okay now that the filler was coming back into my life –

On the soundtrack we hear a few bars of 'The Archers' theme.

VIRGINIA: One stray thing came out of it, though –

NEIL: I started playing golf again.

Just after you left. Found my clubs in the garage. I play twice a week. Said to your mum if my daughter can clear off to Argentina I can go to the links and whack a few balls around. So it's all working out, isn't it? At last? Phil? Your little job?

VIRGINIA: *(To us.)* Weeks later I saw that a Bacon portrait had been sold yet again, for an even higher price. I felt very close to the man it was clear I was going to marry, then, and I wanted to show the article to him – even maybe go to a gallery and look at paintings.

PHIL: I'm just popping out to the Garden Centre to get one of those wooden benches. It'll look nice out there. Or was there something?

VIRGINIA: *(To us.)* I wanted to tell him that was how my face looked to me in the mirror when I came out of surgery but –

PHIL: Unless it's urgent?

VIRGINIA: Urgent? No. It doesn't matter.

PHIL: Sure?

VIRGINIA: Pop out. *(To us.)* The truth about the portrait is that the figure in it is silently screaming and the truth of my marriage would be a silent scream but marriage, like thyroid cancer, is survivable, given the right medication. It's not necessarily fatal. Although you might feel, often, that you are days away from death.

On the soundtrack we hear a modern Tango piece.

VIRGINIA: I lasted two whole months before I made an excuse about staying late at work and went to a *milonga* in a place in Belsize Park that was said to have one of the best dance floors anywhere – you get a bit fanatical about floors – somewhere I didn't think I'd bump into anyone I knew but –

LARRY: Virginia? Is that you? Larry. Accounts? The dance shoes? Remember? In the lift? I hardly recognized you. There's something –

He holds her and they dance a few steps together.

LARRY: – you're dancing differently, too. Holding yourself different.

VIRGINIA: I've been to Buenos Aires.

LARRY: I heard. B.A. *Took off just like that; done a runner to a Tango school,* they said. *Bloody hell,* I thought. *Good for her.* Was it amazing?

VIRGINIA: It was amazing.

LARRY: Did you find a good teacher?

VIRGINIA: I did.

LARRY: Did you fall in love with him?

VIRGINIA: Yes.

LARRY: Did he break your heart?

VIRGINIA: Yes.

LARRY: Of course he did. What's Buenos Aires like?

VIRGINIA: It's everything they say. They think like Italians, speak Spanish and wake up in Paris every day in their heads.

LARRY: Doesn't that sound…?

He tails off wistfully.

VIRGINIA: You've never been?

LARRY: Always thought I might. Then the kids arrived and the next chance I got the wife got sick and money's been a bit tight.

VIRGINIA: You just go the airport and get on a plane.

LARRY: That night – outside the office – I wasn't sure if I should ask you to get in the cab and come to the *milonga* or not. I know how Tango gets people, you see, how it takes over.

VIRGINIA: You're not to blame for me leaving my job and trying to mess my life up.

LARRY: I have a good job and a happy marriage. I really have nothing to complain about but if I didn't have this – if I didn't have Tango – two, three times a week – I'd step in front of a train.

VIRGINIA: You don't mean that.

LARRY: Oh, I mean it.

VIRGINIA turns to us as he walks away.

VIRGINIA: Sometimes there's a shadow you suddenly see on the dance floor. Hear a note from the bandoneon that chills you. There's the moment when the music ends and your partner turns away and you're alone again. Again you're alone. For a moment there's been that connection but it's only been a dance.

Marco wasn't far wrong. Maybe it's not a dance with death exactly but –

Trying to sum it up.

VIRGINIA: The vicar's wife sometimes disappears for a week or so. Nothing's said but everybody in the village knows that she's –

She makes a drinking motion.

VIRGINIA: – he brings her back and it's tight English smiles all around and everybody pretends nothing happened. It's her little thing and Tango would be mine. In the back of everybody's head, though, would be the time I –

She mimes a plane taking off.

VIRGINIA: – I wouldn't be watched as closely as her but *There was that time when our Virginia went a bit Cadbury's Flake on us –*

She twirls a finger at the side of her head, a touch of fear in her voice.

VIRGINIA: I thought I'd landed back on the ground. Maybe I was still falling. Even faster. But I didn't know it yet.

PHIL pulls out his phone.

PHIL: Christ, Vee. They fired Nick Heffernan this morning. Expenses fiddle. I've got Regional. Probationary, of course but this is it. New car. Bigger office. Game on, eh? *Game on.*

VIRGINIA: That was Phil, dad.

NEIL: Good news?

VIRGINIA: He thinks so. I mean Yes.

PHIL: I think we can splash out tonight. How about that new –

A few notes of 'Y Viva Espana' sound on the soundtrack.

PHIL: – *tapas* place on the High Street. You like that kind of stuff, don't you? We should get a move on. Parking's diabolic if we make it any later.

VIRGINIA: I do like that kind of stuff, yes. *(To us.)* I rushed upstairs and threw on the first thing I found.

This –

She pulls the 'English' dress off to reveal the Tango dress she's still wearing but he barely glances at it as he texts on the phone.

PHIL: Not that dress.

VIRGINIA: What?

PHIL: It's – you know –

VIRGINIA: It's –?

PHIL: It's so Tango.

VIRGINIA: So –?

PHIL: And there's the –

He touches his neck where her scar is.

VIRGINIA: I like this dress.

PHIL: But it shows the – you know?

VIRGINIA: The scar? Is that what you want to say? Is that the word you're looking for?

PHIL: I just think you'd be more comfortable in something –

VIRGINIA: More nun-like?

PHIL: That's –

VIRGINIA: My hair – up or down?

PHIL: That's –

VIRGINIA: Is it too Tango like this, too? *(To us.)* I flew upstairs to change again because he didn't want to lose the reservation but I stopped halfway –

On the soundtrack we hear a deconstructed series of notes –

VIRGINIA: I sat under the photograph of my grandfather.

I'll play my mum –

CHRISTA: You're keeping Philip waiting, Virginia.

VIRGINIA: This is important, really important. I have to get this right. Like grandad did. Aren't we here only because he made a huge, huge decision? To leave Vienna before Hitler got there?

CHRISTA: I'd only just got you back again from the operation when you got Tango fever – yes, I'll call it that, don't laugh. I had to keep it together during that terrible time. Your father went to pieces, Phil couldn't really get his head around it, so I had to be – I'll use a word you might use – *implacable.* Someone had to keep pressing on, doing the things that had to be done and you can't rely on men at times like that – they're not made that way.

I said *If I allow myself to think even for a moment that she won't get through this, then she won't.* And just when I thought I had you back off you go. To Buenos Aires, my God. Without stopping to think.

VIRGINIA: Is that a bad thing? Not stopping to think? Maybe?

CHRISTA: What you did terrified me. *It terrified me.*

VIRGINIA: I was scared most of the time too.

CHRISTA: You shouldn't do things that make you feel bad.

VIRGINIA: If they make you feel alive?

CHRISTA: It's impossible to talk to you if you say things like that. I can never get to what really matters. Like *What are you looking for? Who are you looking for?* Aren't you allowed to ask the daughter you love, that?

VIRGINIA: Tango makes me happy. Isn't that enough? For now?

CHRISTA: But are you happy being happy? Some people aren't.

NEIL: It's a great mistake to think life is about making big decisions, like the one you made when you got on that plane. It's the small ones that really matter – they're the ones that add up – like deciding to go into the office every bloody day on that bloody train to bloody Waterloo.

VIRGINIA: Yes daddy but –

NEIL: We're the ones who make the wheels go round. If it means you have to give up something for it –

VIRGINIA: You give up something if you have a passion for something, too. That you have to keep working at. Knowing you might never be as good as you want to be.

PHIL: *(Aggressive.)* Vinny –

VIRGINIA: Phil –

PHIL: Tick tock –

VIRGINIA: I'm wearing this dress tonight.

PHIL: No you're not.

VIRGINIA: I am. There's an Argentinian writer, Borges –

PHIL: Bloody Argentina again?

VIRGINIA: In one of his poems he says that any life is made up of a single moment, the moment in which you find out, once and for all, who you are.

PHIL: Want me to move the reservation up a bit? Half an hour?

VIRGINIA: I don't, no. I want you to tell me that you understand that the body – which as I know better than most people – is a thing of blood and gut and sinew and bone and which can turn against you without warning; that will try to kill you – *kill you* – for no reason you can understand – is also the thing that, when you dance, can bring you closer to Joy than anything else in the world –

PHIL: An hour?

VIRGINIA: – but if you duck that moment or the right muscle doesn't twitch in the right way at the right time, you're lost. You go upstairs to change your dress and unfix your hair when you're told. You stay in Austria and get sent to the camps. I'm fighting for my life here, too, in my own way. I have to get this right.

PHIL has finally taken enough.

PHIL: Do you know why you gave up painting?

VIRGINIA: What?

PHIL: You got to the point where you knew you couldn't get any better. The penny dropped. That was as good as you were going to be. Ever. Like you just said. With this bloody Tango, though, you're never going to get there. There's this style of Tango and that style – you do this step –

He badly mimes a Tango step.

PHIL: Or you do that step –

He mimes another step.

PHIL: You dance this way –

Another step.

PHIL: Or that way –

Another step.

PHIL: – you can always tell yourself you're on the way to getting somewhere without ever having to admit you didn't. That you never will. One more lesson – one more *manguera* or whatever they're called – one more trip to

Buenos Bloody Aires – that's all it's going to take but of course it isn't because this damn thing –

He picks up the bandoneon left on stage by the MUSICIAN.

PHIL: – isn't ever going to be done with you and that's great because you'll never have to admit to yourself what you had to do in the end about your painting. That it's just not there.

Before she can respond.

PHIL: Hang on. You say it's art. I'll give you that, for the sake of argument. It's still a hobby. A pastime. An indulgence. Not something to build your life around. You've got me, if you want me but you should know that I hate the very sound of this damn thing – *(The bandoneon.)* – gasping and wheezing and thumping and making every bugger around you miserable.

He speaks to the MUSICIAN, still off-stage.

PHIL: I'm sorry, pal but it does – *(To VIRGINIA.)* As if being miserable is worth more than being happy. As if it's realer, somehow. I don't want to hurt anybody's feelings but if you're fed up with something why not shut up about it instead of writing a song about it?

NEIL: Phil –

PHIL: I'm sorry – if I don't have my say now I never will and I say the hell with the – what do you call it? – the bandoneon. I say the hell with it and the hell with Tango. I say the hell with you sneaking off to dance it behind my back, like you did the other night – I know you did – I saw the shoes in your handbag. And while we're at it I say the hell with Argentina and Bloody Buenos Bloody Aires – I've never been but I know I'd hate them.

VIRGINIA: If I lost everything now, today, as long as I could get to dance somewhere tonight, it would be all right because it's about being in the moment Borges writes about, moment after moment after moment – some of them dangerous, like with Erik, where you don't know where it'll end up –

PHIL: Hang on. Who's Erik?

VIRGINIA: – but even with him you're not dancing by yourself, you're with another human being who is in his moment, too –

PHIL: Erik who?

VIRGINIA: – and if you have the perfect partner you can do amazing things, together, things that make time stand still –

PHIL: *We're* meant to be partners. That's what all this is about, you and me so how do you think I'm going to feel when you're out every night of the week with somebody else pawing at you –

VIRGINIA: That isn't what it's about. Why do people think that?

PHIL: I'm going to be at home, imagining it; imagining you going off with somebody else –

VIRGINIA: I wouldn't do that.

PHIL: You slept with Diego Maradona or whatever his name was –

VIRGINIA: I lost my head. Once.

PHIL: What the bloody hell is going on with you? *(Hastily.)* Not in Spanish.

VIRGINIA: Watch. No. Do it –

She pushes the chairs aside, tries to cajole him into opening himself up.

VIRGINIA: Walk. That's all you have to do. Just walk. You don't need music. Now we walk together. You lead and I follow.

She puts his hand on her belly.

VIRGINIA: I can even close my eyes and I'm still in touch with you.

She closes her eyes, follows him.

VIRGINIA: You see how good that feels?

She opens her eyes, shapes an abrazo with him.

VIRGINIA: When your feet move my feet go where your feet were –

They move together.

VIRGINIA: It's like a conversation – they're talking to each other and sometimes there's nothing to be said –

She pauses.

VIRGINIA: We wait –

She holds the moment.

VIRGINIA: Then you think of something –

She nudges him and he moves.

VIRGINIA: And I pick it up –

She follows.

VIRGINIA: And we're talking again –

PHIL: Yeah, all right, very illuminating –

He tries to pull away but she doesn't let him go.

VIRGINIA: We're having a conversation but we're speaking with our bodies and sometimes – you're actually not bad at this – there's something special to be said so you do something like this –

She demonstrates an ocho.

VIRGINIA: That's an *ocho* – a figure eight – try it.

PHIL: Bollocks.

VIRGINIA: Try it.

She demonstrates and he performs an ocho.

VIRGINIA: Keep your weight here –

She indicates where he should keep his weight.

VIRGINIA: Try again –

PHIL: Really –

VIRGINIA: Do it.

He does the ocho.

VIRGINIA: When you do that I might add a little decoration to it –

She adds a step.

VIRGINIA: You might do this –

Another step.

VIRGINIA: I might do this –

Another step.

VIRGINIA: This is the *gancho* –

She wraps her leg around his.

VIRGINIA: We're not just talking now, we're telling a story and the great thing about Tango is we're making it up as we go along –

She demonstrates more complicated steps.

VIRGINIA: Imagine if there was music –

PHIL: That bloody thing?

He indicates the bandoneon.

VIRGINIA: What if you let it –

She makes him pause.

VIRGINIA: If you listened –

She still holds the moment.

VIRGINIA: If you got to the moment when you understood that even if you weren't moving you were still dancing –

Still without moving.

VIRGINIA: You're the man – you lead – you're the one who chooses when to break that moment and move again –

Without thinking, PHIL moves and she follows.

VIRGINIA: You see? You see?

PHIL does a couple of the steps that she showed him and more by accident than design, succeeds with them.

VIRGINIA: Look at you.

He stops, perfectly balanced, for the briefest of moments his body shaped like a Tango dancer's.

PHIL: Bollocks.

Abruptly he lets go of her.

PHIL: Are we going or not?

VIRGINIA: You had it. That was –

She's genuinely surprised.

VIRGINIA: Didn't it feel good? You were –

She strikes the male Tango pose he assumed.

PHIL: And I looked a right prat and all.

VIRGINIA: You didn't. Mum, dad, tell him he didn't.

PHIL: It's not for me.

VIRGINIA: What isn't?

PHIL: Leave it there.

VIRGINIA: You could do this.

PHIL: You're out of order now, Vee.

VIRGINIA: You could.

She reaches for his hands to shape an abrazo but he pushes away.

PHIL: Leave it –

She tries to cajole him again.

VIRGINIA: Do it –

She reaches again and he wrenches his hands away this time.

PHIL: I'm telling you –

VIRGINIA: Tell me what? When you could do it – you actually did it –

Again she reaches for him and this time there's real force when he frees himself; so much force that she hurts her wrists.

PHIL: Will you be told? Will you? It's not me.

There's a hint of fear with the anger; as if he's glimpsed a possibility he's too scared to accept.

PHIL: I know what's me and what isn't –

VIRGINIA: Remember the *milonga* we went to?

PHIL: That went on all bloody night?

VIRGINIA: Remember the couple at the end?

PHIL: The fat old woman and the skinny little guy?

83

VIRGINIA: They'd been in the moment with each other for forty or fifty years, moment by moment and were still as much in love as that first moment. Remember –?

She takes him in the old-fashioned abrazo the old couple danced in. Again, she's trying to cajole him by the power of the music; this time with Carlos Gardel's Volvio una noche.

VIRGINIA: *Volvió una noche, no la esperaba,*
Había en su rostro tanta ansiedad
Que tuve miedo de recordarle
Su felonía y su crueldad.

PHIL: Knock it off –

He tries to get free but she resists.

VIRGINIA: *Me dijo humilde: 'Ay, si me perdonas,*
El tiempo aquel otra vez volverá.
La primavera es nuestra vida,
Verás que todo nos sonreirá'

PHIL: I won't tell you again.

She holds him even more tightly.

VIRGINIA: *Mentira, mentira, yo quise decirle,*
Las horas que pasan ya no vuelven más.
Y así mi cariño –

He breaks free and pushes a chair between them.

PHIL: Would you give up Tango? If I asked you?

VIRGINIA: Sometimes I wish I'd never let it into my life. That Larry Lawlor from Accounts had acted on his instinct and not asked me to get in the cab.

PHIL: Who the hell is Larry Lawlor, now?

VIRGINIA: It's so hard. It asks so much. But to even think of giving it up –

PHIL: Would you?

VIRGINIA: Maybe mum's right. Maybe I am one of those people who can't be happy being happy. Not even that's enough. Maybe there is something wrong with me.

PHIL: I'm asking you straight. Would you give it the –

He gestures with his elbow.

PHIL: – if I asked?

VIRGINIA: Maybe there's something wrong with everybody who has a passion for something but if I go back upstairs and take this dress off – if I settle for *Just the Job* –

She tries to move the chair but he grabs for it at the same time and it falls to the ground.

PHIL: It's a simple question. Tango or me. What's it to be? Virginiarini?

VIRGINIA: There is something only I can say. No one else in the history of the world has said it or will be able to say it. I will let nothing get in the way of it being said. By me. *By me.*

PHIL: So all right, then. All right.

They're facing each other, breathless over the chair. Then he carefully picks it up, sets it down again and heads away.

CHRISTA: It would have been such a lovely, lovely wedding.

On the screen we see Virginia in a wedding gown with JUST THE JOB underneath it.

VIRGINIA: I know, mum.

CHRISTA: You would have been *kind* of happy –

VIRGINIA: Is that what I have to settle for?

CHRISTA: If it is, my poor darling – if it is…?

The image disappears as VIRGINIA picks up her backpack.

VIRGINIA: *(To us.)* It's a simple story and we're very near the end of it. For now –

She sits on one chair.

VIRGINIA: Heathrow –

She sits on another chair.

VIRGINIA: The plane –

She sits on another chair.

VIRGINIA: Buenos Aires.

The 'Malena' 78 RPM record plays again as THE OLD MAN shuffles his steps around the boombox.

VIRGINIA: He was there again. Of course he was. Marco was somewhere, too. But that was over.

She tosses the backpack into the wings.

VIRGINIA: I'm sharing an apartment in San Telmo with two people I met on the plane. Yes, they're here to learn Tango. When my money runs out – well – I'll decide what to do, then. And before you say anything – I know I've ruined my life – but in a good way, if you know what I mean.

She lights a cigarette.

VIRGINIA: In the Chacarita Cemetary is a statue of Carlos Gardel, who people think of as the greatest Tango singer of all time –

In silhouette the male actor stands three quarters on, with his hand in front of him, fingers of his right hand open.

VIRGINIA: There's a tradition that you pay your respects or – I suppose – ask for his blessing – by lighting a cigarette for him and –

She lights a cigarette, takes it from her lips and places it between his fingers.

VIRGINIA: – a very un-English thing to do but then –

A capella, she sings the Spanish words of 'Malena'. She sings with attack and passion – as if this song is the celebration of the person she's come here to be, without reserve; a manifesto for how she's going to live with fierceness and joy no matter where it takes her.

VIRGINIA: *(Sings.) Malena canta el tango como ninguna*
Y en cada verso pone su corazón,
A yuyo de suburbio su voz perfuma,
Malena tiene pena de bandoneón.

Speaking, she translates some of the verse.

VIRGINIA: Malena sings the tango like no one else
And into each verse she pours her heart –

(Sings.) Tal vez allá, en la infancia, su voz de alondra
Tomó ese tono oscuro de callejón,
O acaso aquel romance que sólo nombra
Cuando se pone triste con el alcohol.

Speaking again.

VIRGINIA: Perhaps in her childhood she sang like a bird –

(Sings.) Malena canta el tango con voz de sombra,
Malena tiene pena de bandoneón.

Speaking.

VIRGINIA: Malena sings the tango –

One day maybe I'll dream in Spanish, too.

Mist starts to drift on stage and on the soundtrack we hear a keening
wind start to blow as the male actor leaves and she's alone on stage.

VIRGINIA: Right at the end of Argentina is Ushuaia, the
southernmost town in the world. I'm going to go there one
day.

ON THE SCREEN we see images of ice and snow and mountainous
peaks disappearing into the distance under a huge sky.

VIRGINIA: You look out at the ocean and beyond it there's
Antarctica, a whole new continent, my thirties and my
forties and my fifties waiting for me – the whole of the rest
of my life now that my twenties are nearly over –

The MUSICIAN heads back to the music stand.

VIRGINIA: It started with a Tango in a hall in North London
and it ends – for now – but just for now – because there's
all of Antarctica and everyplace else to explore –

She gestures at the MUSICIAN, who starts to play.

VIRGINIA: – it ends in a Tango bar in La Boca where they say
Tango began – working illegally, for tips and for a chance
to watch the greatest *tangueros* and *tanqueras* every night –

She steps off the stage and starts to collect glasses from the cabaret
tables at the front of the auditorium.

VIRGINIA: – learning about Tango *Salon* and Club Tango
and *Fantasia* and *Canyque* and Nuevo and Orillero – all
the different ways to make this dance and to listen to the
arguments about them as if it matters more than life itself
– more even than football – and to walk home at four in
the morning with my dance shoes in my hand and my bare
feet on the pavement which is still warm from the heat of
the day and my head, my head, my head filled with –

The MUSICIAN plays a heart-felt, emphatic, life-affirming Tango that contains in it all the pleasure of dance. VIRGINIA finishes her work, takes off her shoes, massages her aching feet, picks up her sweater. She heads to the street to wait for the bus, body still reverberating with the music she's heard all night.

She sits at the bus-stop, replete and happy. The music still doesn't let her go. It pulls her to her feet and she dances with the shoes in her hand, trailing the sweater. The male actor dances with her for a fleeting moment and then leaves as she spins around and around, complete in herself, alone on stage under a caption which says what the music and the movement and the play have been trying to say.

CAPTION: Be brave…

Take wing…

The lights fade on the image of that body ecstatically moving in space and time and we

End.